General Jan Christian Smuts
The Debunking of a Myth

by

Stephen Mitford Goodson

Frontispiece: Smuts in uniform of Lieutenant-General World War I

December 2012
First Edition

August 2013
Second Edition

July 2017
Third Edition

ISBN Number 1717060137

By the Same Author

An Illustrated Guide to Adolf Hitler
and the Third Reich

A History of Central Banking and
the Enslavement of Mankind

Inside the South African Reserve Bank
Its Origins and Secrets Exposed

Rhodesian Prime Minister Ian Smith The
Debunking of a Myth

Hendrik Frensch Verwoerd South Africa's
Greatest Prime Minister

The Genocide of the Boers

Dedication

Dedicated with affection and gratitude to the memory of
Jason Collett who edited this work.

28 November 2012

True glory consists in doing what deserves to be written; in writing what deserves to be read. – *Pliny the Elder*

Contents

Foreword

Jan Christian Smuts was one of the most influential people of the 20th century. Not only for South Africa, but influential in world history. For us to *understand the times*, it is vital that we understand the role played by Jan Smuts and why.

A graduate of both Stellenbosch and Cambridge Universities, Smuts was recruited to the globalist agenda of Cecil John Rhodes and the De Beers Mining Company.

As State Attorney for the South African Republic, Smuts played a pivotal role in the Transvaal delegation which led to South Africa being torn apart by the ruinous Anglo-Boer War. Smuts also played a key role in bringing South Africa into both the First and Second World Wars, on the British side.

Smuts drafted foundational documents for both the League of Nations and the United Nations and served in Lloyd George's War Cabinet during World War I. General Smuts also played a key-role in deposing the extremely popular South African Prime Minister, General James Barry Hertzog, in September 1939 in order to lead South Africa into the Second World War. Jan Smuts then secretly shipped all the gold available in South Africa (20 million pounds) to America, on board the US Battle Cruiser, *Quincy*, to fund Britain's War.

Considering his critical role in three of the most ruinous wars our country has ever been involved in, it is surprising how little is known of this intriguing man.

Stephen Mitford Goodson has done us all a tremendous service by lifting the veil of secrecy on so many facts and facets of this extraordinary life, which has been so skillfully concealed from the public. Along with his outstanding biography on *Hendrik Verwoerd – South Africa's Greatest Prime Minister*, this new book on Jan Smuts is essential reading for anyone wanting to understand not only South African, but world history in the 20th century. You will be astounded at the role played by this extraordinary lawyer, politician and military leader and how his influence continues to affect us to this day.

Dr. Peter Hammond
Frontline Fellowship

Introduction

Jan Christian Smuts was a dominant figure on the world stage of politics for over 50 years. He led commandos in the Anglo-Boer War. In World War I he was a member of the British Imperial War Cabinet and helped to create the Royal Air Force. In World War II he became a Field Marshal. He was the only person to sign the treaties ending both the First and Second World Wars. He was central to the establishment of the League of Nations. He later urged the formation of a new international organisation for peace, the United Nations and wrote the preamble to its charter. He was the only person to sign the charters of both the League of Nations and the United Nations Organisation. He helped to establish the British Commonwealth. In 2004 he was named by voters in a poll held by the South African Broadcasting Corporation as one of the top ten Greatest South Africans of all time occupying the position of sixth.

Who was General Smuts and what influence did he have on world events? Was he a loyal servant of the South African people, and in particular the Boers/Afrikaners, or did he have a different agenda, which served other masters?

In 1949 Smuts was asked why he did not write his personal memoirs as Winston Churchill had done. He replied that "I know too much" and that he would not write any memoirs, not only because he was too busy, but mainly he admitted because the documents used by historians as their source material "do not represent the full truth" and that if the truth was divulged, it would gravely disturb "the accepted version of events". [1] This book probes into these issues and attempts to reveal the real General Smuts and the many facets and facts of his life, which he so skillfully concealed from the public for over half a century.

Stephen Mitford Goodson

---

1   J.J. McCord, *South African Struggle*, J.H. DeBussy, Pretoria, 1952, 385.

Chapter I

Youth

Jan Christian Smuts was born in the district of Riebeeck West (45 miles or 72 km north east of Cape Town) at the house Bovenplaats on his parents' farm Ongedund on 24 May 1870. He was born on Queen Victoria's birthday and in 1938 remarked, "It is my luck to have been born on the same day" [2]. His father, Jacobus Abraham, was a prosperous cattle and wheat farmer and a member of the Cape Parliament.

Smuts grew up as a farm boy and his mother, Catharina (née DeVries), taught him the elements of reading and writing. At the age of 12 he attended his first school, Die Ark, which was run by T.C. Stoffberg, at Riebeeck West. His precociousness and intelligence enabled him to advance quickly through the classes. He had a prodigious capacity for reading coupled with a photographic memory. In 1886 he went to Victoria College, [3] Stellenbosch, where he studied High Dutch, Ancient Greek, German and science. He managed to learn all the declensions, conjugations and irregular verbs of Greek grammar in six days.[4] He graduated with first class honours in literature and science. It was during this time that he met Sybella Margaretha "Isie" Krige [5] the daughter of a leading farmer. They married on 30 April 1897.

2   P.B. Blanckenberg, *The Thoughts of General Smuts,* Juta & Co., Limited, Cape Town, 1951, 41.
3   The status of the Victoria College was changed to the University of Stellenbosch on 2 April 1918. W.K. Hancock in his biography of Smuts, *The Sanguine Years*, describes the almost idyllic life of the students at that time as follows: "Victoria College, Stellenbosch, stamped its enduring imprint upon the mind of Smuts. The small teaching body, hardly more than half a dozen men, covered a wide curriculum; but the students also were few and carefully sifted for quality. Teachers and students were able in consequence to enjoy close contact with each other and – despite an essay that Smuts wrote in 1889, denouncing the hurry of modern life – they were able to work in an atmosphere of leisure." As quoted in C. Fensham, *Ou Hoofgebou, 'n Eeu Oud*, Kaapstad, 1986, 53-54. 80 years later the author studied in the same building as Smuts - Die Ou Hoofgebou - English, Latin and Roman-Dutch law.
4   S.G. Millin, *General Smuts*, Faber and Faber Limited, London, 1936, 15.
5   Isie Krige was a very unassuming woman. The author's English schoolmistress at Western Province Preparatory School, Miss Dorothy Saint Hill, who was a Girl Guide Captain, once related the following incident regarding Mrs. Smuts. In about 1946 she held a camp on Smuts' farm Doornkloof, near Irene, Pretoria. At the end of the week she went to the house to thank Mrs. Smuts and opened the back door. On her knees wearing an apron was a woman with curlers in her hair scrubbing the kitchen floor. She asked if she could please speak to the 'madam'. To her embarrassment she was told that she was speaking to the madam!

An Ebden scholarship worth £100[6] gave Smuts the opportunity to read law at Christ's College, Cambridge from 1891-93. The scholarship was worth only half the usual amount of £200 and the additional £100 was only granted on 28 July 1894. In the interim Smuts was forced to borrow the deficit in funds from a sympathetic professor. Smuts passed with a double first (double cum laude) in the law tripos and became the first student to do so in the 600 year history of Cambridge University. The title of his treatise was *Law, a Liberal Study*.

Oxford [7] and Cambridge [8] have always been the favourite recruiting grounds of bright students for employment as British intelligence agents. It is the author's contention, as will be confirmed by Smuts' behaviour on a consistent basis and by subsequent events, that he was recruited as a secret agent, while he was studying at Cambridge.[9]

Smuts was a devotee of Walt Whitman's theory of synthesis and during this period he wrote an unpublished work *Walt Whitman: A Study in the Evolution of Personality*. According to his last private secretary, Piet Beukes,[10] Smuts was also influenced by the works of Goethe, Shakespeare and Shelley. Smuts turned down a professorship at Cambridge and for a short while practised as a barrister at the Middle Temple, one of the four Inns of Court, in London.

Present day South Africa at that time consisted of two independent Boer republics, the *Oranje Vrij Staat* (Orange Free State) and the *Zuid-Afrikaansche Republiek* (South African Republic) and two British self-governing colonies, the Cape Colony and Natal.

6   Alfred Ebden, who came from the Eastern Cape, was a spokesman for a group of supporters of Sir Alfred Milner. P. C. Swanepoel, *General Jan Smuts Was He on Our Side in the Anglo-Boer War?*, Self-published, Pretoria, 2012, 47.
7   Between 1909-1913 while Prince Felix Felixovich Yusupov was studying at Oxford University, he was recruited together with his friend, Oswald Rayner, by the British Secret Intelligence Service. When it was learnt that Grigori Rasputin was strongly influencing Tsarina Alexandra to terminate the war with Germany in late 1916, Rayner was sent by British intelligence to carry out the assassination of Rasputin with the co-operation of Prince Yusupov. S.Goodson, Murdering the Czars: The Rothschild Connection, *The Barnes Review*, Washington D.C., Vol. XX, No. 5. September/October 2014, 38-40.
8   The recruitment of Cambridge students Kim Philby, Guy Burgess, Donald Maclean and Anthony Blunt by Soviet Russia's secret service is one of the better known examples of such methods of intelligence gathering. Three weeks before he died on 19 July 2005 the author met the former leader of the British National Party (BNP), John Tyndall, at his home in Hove, Sussex. Tyndall expressed a deep concern that the BNP had been infiltrated by MI5. Four years later the BNP achieved an electoral breakthrough when two of its candidates were elected to the European Parliament. Thereafter the BNP went into a steep decline and eventual oblivion under its leader, Nick Griffin. Griffin is a graduate of the University of Cambridge.
9   http://www.renegadetribune.com/heaven-hell-true-story-whites-south-africa/
10 P. Beukes, *The Holistic Smuts A Study in Personality*, Human & Rousseau, Cape Town, 1989, 45.

In June 1895 Smuts returned to the Cape Colony. His ascetic behaviour and his abrasive and brusque manner prevented him from obtaining sufficient briefs, and in order to survive he turned to newspaper reporting, and in particular the debates in the Cape Parliament. H.C. Armstrong in *Grey Steel J.C. Smuts A Study in Arrogance* writes that Smuts "…could not hobnob with other junior counsel, do the usual passing the time of day things they did, playing cards, swapping drinks, sitting in the casual, sociable manner of Cape Town to talk by the hour. He was constitutionally unable to get on to familiar or intimate terms with the other men. He had a hesitating and reserved manner, with a haughty look, and his pale blue eyes looked past or through people and held them at arm's length, so that juniors liked him as little as the Cambridge undergraduates had".[11]

Smuts then joined the Afrikaner Bond, led by Jan Hendrik Hofmeyr, which had an informal alliance with Cecil John Rhodes who governed the Cape Colony. Both Hofmeyr and Rhodes were freemasons, with the former having held the position of Grand Master of the Lodge de Goede Hoop. Rhodes was a speculator, who had a amassed a fortune after amalgamating the diamond mines in Kimberley in the Northern Cape. Rhodes had obtained finance from the Rothschild Bank, and although he had his own views regarding the political development of Southern Africa, he would always remain a servant of the Rothschild interests.[12]

Rhodes first became aware of Smuts in February 1891[13] after the latter had been chosen to reply to a speech he had given to the students at Stellenbosch. Rhodes was so impressed with Smuts' reply that he asked Hofmeyr to keep an eye on Smuts for future employment. A little later he said to Alfred Harmsworth, Lord Rothermere, the newspaper baron: "Keep an eye on that young

11   H.C. Armstrong, *Grey Steel J.C. Smuts A Study in Arrogance*, Arthur Barkers Ltd, London, 1937, 36. According to P. Beukes, *op.cit.*, 18, Armstrong's biography made Smuts "angry and upset".
12   H.R. Abercrombie, *The Secret History of South Africa or Sixty five years in the Transvaal*, Central News Agency Ltd, Johannesburg, 1952, 205. When Ewald Esselen, Attorney General of the ZAR, asked Rhodes why he did not cut diamonds in South Africa, the latter replied: "This is one of the things **my masters, the Rothschilds, will not let me do**".
13   Calendar of the Victoria College, Stellenbosch Session 1891-92, Stellenbosch Public School, Report and Class-Lists, 1890-91. In the beginning of the present term the Hon. C.J. Rhodes, Premier of the Colony, paid a visit to the College, accompanied by the Hon. The Colonial Secretary, the Hon. Treasurer of the Colony, the Hon. The Attorney General and the Members of Parliament for the district. After visiting the various departments and laboratories, Mr. Rhodes addressed the students in the Hall.

man, **he will do big service for the Empire before he has finished**".[14]
Smuts greatly admired both Rhodes[15] and his imperial ambitions,
which he supported whole-heartedly. Having failed to succeed
as an advocate, Smuts obtained employment as a junior legal
counsel to the De Beers diamond mining company and in this
manner became drawn into advancing the Rothschilds' interests.

On 9 October 1895 at a meeting of the De Beers Political and
Debating Society in the Town Hall at Kimberley, Smuts openly
declared his support for Rhodes. Biographer F.S. Crafford
describes Smuts' devotion to the ideals of Rhodes as follows:
"Little did he know that the spirit of Rhodes would be with him
for the rest of his days and that in time, he, Jan Smuts, would be
called Rhodes Recidivus. Little did he know that he and Rhodes
were kindred spirits".[16]

---

14   H.C. Armstrong, *op.cit.*, 45.
15   *Ibid.*, 46. Carroll Quigley, *Tragedy and Hope*, The Macmillan Company, New York, 1966, 137
      describes Smuts as having been "a vigorous supporter".
16   F.S. Crafford, *Jan Smuts: A Biography*, Doubleday, Doran & Co., Inc., New York, 1943, 20.

Chapter II

BUILD-UP TO THE ANGLO-BOER WAR

In 1886 gold was discovered on the Witwatersrand. On the announcement of the discovery of this gold, General Piet Joubert, Commandant General of the *Zuid-Afrikaansche Republiek* (ZAR) declared: "Instead of rejoicing, you should rather weep, because that gold will cause our land to be drenched in blood".[17] This discovery created enormous interest amongst speculators and, in particular, the Rothschild dynasty, which represented the foremost banking group of the age and was headed at that time by the three brothers, Nathan, Alfred and Leopold Rothschild. They were extremely anxious to obtain control of these vast goldfields in order to further their monopoly on the gold standard system of banking, a system, which allows for the creation of money out of nothing and the sale of this credit to gullible borrowers (mainly governments). The leader of the ZAR, where all the goldmines were situated, was a resolute and Biblically guided Boer leader, President Stephanus Johannes Paulus Krüger, also known as *Oom* (Uncle) Paul. In his inaugural speech on 9 May 1883, President Krüger enunciated the principle that the natural wealth of the country must contribute to the industrial and general development of the State to secure its future.

The Jewish mining magnates, such as George Albu, Barney Barnato, Alfred Beit, Solly Joel , Sammy Marks and Lionel Phillips, were attempting to unseat Krüger by using a pretext that the *uitlanders* (foreigners) - who were the workers and speculators on the mines and who outnumbered the Boers by about two to one - were being denied their democratic right to have the vote. The Boers' distrust of the *uitlanders* dated back to the treacherous support that the English-speaking miners in the Eastern Transvaal had given to the British in 1877 during the First Anglo-Boer War (1877-1881). One of the fronts used was called the South African League, but as Professor John A. Hobson, the English economist, observed, "only a small minority of British outlanders would have been willing definitely to accept the franchise upon the

---

17   J.J. McCord, *op.cit.*, 99.

President Paul Kruger of the *Zuid-Afrikaansche Republiek* (1883-1900)
who was forced to defend his country from the depredations of the
Rothschild controlled British Empire on three occasions.

conditions indicated by Sir Alfred Milner at Bloemfontein
and afterwards at Cape Town", and that there was "a strong
prima facie case for the view that "the franchise was entirely a
sham grievance." [18] He also noted that a "large number of
non-British outlanders [were] mostly Russian, Polish and
German Jews, with roving propensities and no strongly rooted
attachment to an old country". In a letter to Sir Alfred Beit,
mining magnate Sir Lionel Phillips remarked that " ... as to
the franchise, do not think many people care a fig about it". [19]

18 J.A. Hobson, *The War in South Africa, Its Causes and Effects*, James Nisbet and Co. Limited,
    London, 1900, 66-70.
19 J.J. McCord, *op.cit.*, 152.

On 7 August 1895 the British government, which until the previous year had been under the moderate and Liberal administration of Prime Minister William Gladstone, was defeated. The new Conservative government adopted a decidedly confrontational agenda. On 29 December 1895 a force of six hundred soldiers under the command of Dr. Leander Starr Jameson, a confidant of Rhodes, crossed the border into WesternTransvaal and set out for Johannesburg. A planned uprising of *uitlanders* did not take place and four days later Jameson's force was routed. Rhodes's involvement was revealed and he was forced to resign as premier of the Cape Colony.

Despite his support for Pax Britannica, Smuts appeared to be deeply disillusioned by his hero's underhand behaviour towards his Afrikaner brethren.[20] However, Lieutenant General Piet Swanepoel[21] believes that this disillusionment was faked and that Smuts' emigration to the Transvaal "was a carefully planned move to infiltrate the South African Republic's governing organs and to weaken it from the inside". [22] After failing to secure a lectureship in law at the South African College in Cape Town in March 1896, Smuts departed for Johannesburg on 20 January 1897. Once again his aloofness and inability to interact socially prevented him from obtaining sufficient legal work. He often forgot the names of people and used the technique of asking a person's surname, and then replying, "No ,I know that. What is your first name?"

On 29 January 1897 in an article in *The Transvaal Critic* Smuts was accused of receiving funds from Rhodes. The magazine stated that "Mr. Advocate Smuts, enjoys anything but an 'envoy'-able reputation in the Colony, for it is notorious that he was on Mr. Rhodes' 'bounty' list a short while ago … " [23] Smuts refrained from suing the author of the article, Leopold Hess, in either a civil or criminal court.

---

20 N. Levi, *Jan Smuts*, Longmans Green and Co., London, 1917, 34.
21 Lieutenant General Piet Swanepoel (1928-) was a detective for 22 years and an intelligence officer for 15 years in the South African Police. He played a key role in the establishment of the Bureau for State Security (BOSS) in 1969. He is the author of ten books, including two on the secret activities of the CIA in South Africa.
22 P. C. Swanepoel , *op.cit.*, 141.
23 *Ibid.*, 45.

Lieutenant General Sir William Butler (1838-1910), who was commander in chief in South Africa in 1898, described the *uitlanders* as "probably the most corrupt, immoral and untruthful assemblage of beings in the world".

In October 1897 the Secretary for the Colonies, Joseph Chamberlain, tried to insidiously claim suzerainty over the Transvaal Republic, which suzerainty was one of the articles of the Pretoria Convention of 1881, with the sole qualification that the British government had the right of refusing to sanction treaties with foreign states and certain native tribes.[24] Professor Westlake, QC, LLD of Cambridge University and the Institute of International Law concluded that "the contention of Chamberlain that a Suzerainty exists is absolutely invalid and contrary alike to the obvious meaning of the London Convention of 1884 and to the rules of interpretation of the Law of the Nations". [25]

---

24   J.J. McCord, *op.cit.*, 79-81.
25   *Ibid.*, 87.

There was much corruption in Krüger's government, particularly in the state monopolies and the dynamite concession. A visiting American described it as a "Calvinist Tammany".[26] In May 1898 Chief Justice John Gilbert Kotzé, a previous presidential rival of Krüger in the election of 1893, was summarily dismissed for attempting to disregard legislation, which the President alleged had complied with the Constitution. This dispute had arisen as a result of the government losing a mining case which resulted in the loss of over £330,000 and Krüger wanting to overrule the Chief Justice's decision by *besluit* (decision). Kotzé wanted to protect the Court's independence by being allowed to test, in the American way, all legislative acts, but Krüger refused.[27] This decision of Krüger was supported by Smuts in a legal opinion. Smuts became friendly with Hans Malan, chief of the Roads Department. He later introduced Smuts to Piet Grobler who was the nephew and private secretary of President Krüger. Grobler in turn introduced Smuts to the president. Krüger was initially against the appointment of Smuts as State Attorney, but was prevailed upon to do so by Commandant-General Piet Joubert, who happened to be one of the many senior Boers, who was a freemason. On 8 June 1898 at the age of 28 Smuts was appointed, even though he was still a British subject and two years below the age at which such appointments were made, at an annual salary of £2,250. He began a ruthless clean-up of the Krüger administration, which included placing the detective force directly under his control,[28] introduction of measures to prevent illicit gold dealing and eradication of abuses in the liquor trade. However, a leery Krüger continued to describe him as a *schelm* (Dutch for a devious character).[29] In later life Smuts was known as *slim* (clever) *Jannie*.

The mine owners started to reach a rapprochement with the ZAR government, but Milner did everything in his powers to sow discord and enmity.[30] Nothing would deflect Milner from his aim to ensure "British mastery of South Africa" from "Cape to Zambezi".[31]

26   H.C. Armstrong, *op.cit.*, 72.
27   S.G. Millin, *op.cit.*, 69-70.
28   *Ibid.*, 77.
29   P.J. Pretorius, *Volksverraad*, Libanon-Uitgewers, Mosselbaai, Western Cape, 1996, 58.
30   J.J. McCord, *op.cit.*, 223.
31   *Ibid.*, 227.

Sir William Conyngham Greene, the British agent in Pretoria,
with whom Smuts held unauthorised and secret discussions.

Notwithstanding the fact that Smuts was State Attorney and
that foreign affairs were the responsibility of the State Secretary,
Smuts maintained a friendly and confidential relationship with
the Acting British Agent in Pretoria, Edmund Fraser, and later
also with the permanent British Agent, Sir Conyngham Greene.[32]
These secret meetings were highly irregular. On 21 February
1899 Fraser informed Milner by letter that Smuts would be
visiting Cape Town in early March. There is strong circumstantial
evidence that while Smuts was in Cape Town he secretly met
with Milner.[33] Smuts' biographer Sarah Millin also mentions
Milner's attempts to meet Smuts.[34]

---

32   P. C. Swanepoel , *op.cit.*, 57.
33   *Ibid.*, 55-60.
34   S.G. Millin, *op.cit.*, 84. Later Smuts would become a close friend of Milner, particularly
     when he served with the latter in the Imperial War Cabinet from 1917 to 1918.

At a conference in Bloemfontein on 30 May 1899 matters came to a head between Krüger and the belligerent British High Commissioner, Sir Alfred Milner. Seven days prior to this meeting Milner sent a letter marked Very Secret to Lord Selborne, the Under-Secretary of State for the Colonies, proving that the franchise issue was only a pretext when he wrote "we shall fill the land with troops" so that "they put themselves in the wrong and become the aggressors". [35] Smuts attended as Krüger's adviser.[36] The conference got off to a poor start when Milner refused to shake Krüger's outstretched hand. President Steyn was aghast at the rudeness and uncouthness of Milner.[37] In order to appease the British and their controllers, the Rothschilds, Krüger, on the advice of Smuts, made one concession after the other. [38] He offered to reduce the residence qualification for the franchise from 14 to seven years, even though it would result in the Boers being outnumbered by two to one. Eventually Krüger "bowing his head between his big red hands, hot tears streaming down his bearded cheeks" [39] burst out in anguish "It is my country that you want!" [40] Milner then broke off the conference after three days, as he did not want Krüger to make any more concessions, which would lead to peace and deny him the ability to incite a future crisis. Shortly thereafter Milner described Smuts as "Krüger's brilliant state attorney". [41]

On 19 August 1899 Krüger offered to reduce the residency period even more to five years, but the cold-fish Milner, whose point of view was "reform or war", [42] was unmoved. On 26 August 1899 Chamberlain demanded a Commission of Enquiry, which the Boers accepted. On 8 September Chamberlain withdrew his own proposal and instead demanded a five year franchise without the

35   J.J. Peacock, *The Heel of the British Boot: The Deeper Meaning of the Second Anglo-Boer War*, Self-published, Cape Town, 2001, 4.
36   Although Paul Krüger fully understood English, he never spoke it, hence the need for an interpreter. There are two occasions when he did give a speech in English – once to the striking miners in Barberton and on the second occasion when he addressed the *uitlanders* in Johannesburg after the Jameson Raid. He started his latter speech with the words: "Robbers, liars, thieves …" Krüger was fluent in a number of African languages, including Sotho, Tswana and Venda.
37   J.J. McCord, *op.cit.*, 213.
38   It is a noteworthy fact that any nation, which contravenes the Rothschild banking system is soon marked down for destruction, and concessions only serve to hasten that process. In subsequent years we have seen that Adolf Hitler, Benito Mussolini, Hideki Tojo, Slobodan Milosevic, Saddam Hussein and Muammar Gadaffi have been eliminated by the Rothschild proxies of the USA and Britain, notwithstanding all the concessions which they made.
39   P.J. Pretorius, *op.cit.*, 62.
40   R. Kraus, *Old Master Thereof Jan Christian Smuts*, E.P. Dutton & Co. Inc., New York, 1944, 92.
41   S.G. Millin, *op.cit.*, 84.
42   T. Pakenham, *The Boer War*, Jonathan Ball Publishers, London, 1979, 68.

safeguards of the London Convention. This the Boers refused and on 22 September 1899 Chamberlain suspended the pseudo-negotiations and said that the British government would formulate its own proposals for a final settlement, which would be communicated in a later dispatch. "This was an ultimatum." [43] If the Boers did not submit, they would be compelled to do so by force of arms.

Smuts together with Francis William Reitz, the State Secretary, wrote a pamphlet *Een Eeuw van Onrecht* (A Century of Wrong).[44] The preface was written by social reformer and imperialist, William Thomas Stead and was distributed in Europe for propaganda purposes. However, General Swanepoel is of the opinion that the pamphlet may have been written in order to provoke the Boers into action.[45] Meanwhile in an act of provocation and in contravention of the London Convention of 28 January 1884 which had relinquished British suzerainty over the ZAR, the British started to transport more troops from England to South Africa. Some of the Boer military leaders like Koos de la Rey and Louis Botha were reluctant about going to war. In particular General Piet Joubert was very much against a war and not only held meetings, but did all he could to prevent hostilities.[46] However, others were inspired by memories of their resounding defeat of the British at Majuba on 27 February 1881 and adopted a more belligerent stance.

On 22 September 1899 in a cable marked Secret and Personal, Chamberlain wrote to Milner as follows: "Cabinet unanimous and resolves to see the matter through. All preparations for expeditionary force will be proceeded with as quickly as possible, but without public announcement at present. Our proposal for settlement [read ultimatum] will be agreed on next week, and if forwarded by mail will allow four weeks' interval for reinforcements which are now on their way to arrive".[47]

---

43   J.J. McCord, *op.cit.*, 265.
44   R. Kraus, *op.cit.*, 92. Dr. Josef Goebbels, Reich Minister of Public Enlightenment and Propaganda, frequently referred to this document during the "Afrikaans Hour" on the Zeesen radio station. This was the same station from which William Joyce, "Lord Haw Haw", broadcast during World War II. The author's grandmother, who lived in Germiston and was nine years old in 1899, once told me that it was a commonly held view in the Transvaal that the Jews had started the Anglo-Boer War.
45   P. C. Swanepoel , *op.cit.*, 63-64.
46   H.R. Abercrombie, *op.cit.*, 134.
47   J.J. Peacock, *op.cit.*, 5.

Just before the war started treaties were drawn up with France, Germany and Portugal, which prevented them from giving any assistance to the Boer republics without Britain's consent, thus ensuring the Boers' isolation.[48] "It was an international game of grab played on the moral level of gangsters, and Britain with her sea power, and the use of Germany, was assured of the neutrality of Europe in the war that was to be waged against the republics in the corrupt, cynical and brutal spirit of the Old World. A great portion, if not the majority, of the public on the Continent of Europe, also a big minority in Britain, were against this imperialist war, but they had no power to stop it". [49]

The Rothschild's point man Smuts, who was in charge of legal affairs, and thus perfectly placed to act as an *agent provocateur*,[50] & [51] drafted an ultimatum on 9 October 1899 demanding "Immediate withdrawal of Her Majesty's forces". [52] The full text reads as follows:

Sir,

In the name of the Government of the South African Republic I have the honour to bring to your information that this Government, with an eye to the breaking off of friendly relations by Her Majesty's Government, as shown by the constant bringing up of troops to the borders of the Republic, and the sending of war reinforcements from all parts of the British Empire, herewith informs you that unless they receive within forty-eight hours an assurance,

---

48   *Ibid.*, 5-6.
49   J.J. McCord, *op.cit.*, 248.
50   W.B. Worsfold, *Lord Milner's Work in South Africa From its Commencement in 1897 to the Peace of Vereeniging in 1902, Containing Hitherto Unpublished Information*, London, John Murray, 1906, 574. Smuts' role as an agent provocateur is confirmed, when Smuts is cited as stating **"I am one of those, who as members of the government of the South African Republic, provoked the war in England"**.
51   P. C. Swanepoel , *op.cit.*, 44 where he cites Dr. H.J.G. Kamffer, who states in his thesis *Om Een Scherpe Oog in 't zeil te houden, Die Geheime Diens in die Zuid-Afrikaanse Republiek* that "The implication was that Smuts was indirectly accused of having played the role of a double agent".
52   *The Times History of the War in South Africa*, Vol. 1, 354. See also J.C. Smuts (Son), *Jan Christian Smuts*, Cassell & Company Ltd, Cape Town, 1952, 46; T. Pakenham, *op.cit.*, 565 quotes J.D. Kestell, *Through Shot and Flame*, 1903, 310-12, where the latter states that Smuts 'provoked the war' and M. Hugo, *Die Kruger Ultimatum* , Bienedell Uitgewers, Pretoria, 93. In a speech he gave towards the end of his life, Smuts claimed that "the declaration of war by the Transvaal Republic was one of the great heroic acts of the past and that conditions would have been a thousand times worse if the Boer people had remained paralysed before the British threat". P.B. Blanckenberg, *op.cit.*, 182-183.

1. that the troops on the border of this Republic shall be instantly withdrawn;

2. that all reinforcements which have arrived in South Africa since 1 June 1889, shall be removed within a reasonable time;

3. that Her Majesty's troops which are now on the high seas shall not be landed in any port of South Africa – my Government will consider such action of Her Majesty's Government as a formal declaration of war, and will not hold itself responsible for the consequences thereof.

By issuing the ultimatum, Smuts had cast the Transvaal Republic in the role of aggressor and played into the enemy's hands. In response Lord Lansdowne, Secretary of War, wrote to Chamberlain as follows: "Accept my felicitations, I don't think Krüger could have played your cards better than he has … My soldiers are in ecstasies". [53]

---

53 J.J. Peacock, *op.cit.*, 6.

Chapter III

ANGLO-BOER WAR

While the principal objective of the Rothschilds in starting this war was to secure control of the gold mines, a more sinister purpose was also present. As a result of technical and scientific advances in the late nineteenth century, there had been large increases in productivity and a rise in living standards. Between 1870 and 1900 economic output *per caput* in Great Britain rose by 500%. There had also been very few wars during this period and Great Britain's national debt had been in decline since 1887. A war would thus be very beneficial to the profits of those bankers, who specialised in financing governments. The Anglo-Boer War cost £222 million or £25 billion in to-day's values and resulted in the addition of £132 million to the British national debt and a consequent increase in the profits of the Rothschild Bank. [54]

The hubristic British expected a brief campaign or tea-time war, and in anticipation thereof issued the Queen's South Africa Medal, a service decoration, with the years 1899-1900 engraved on it. These dates had to be removed when it transpired that they were opposed by a formidable foe, and instead the war lasted for two years and eight months from 11 October 1899 to 31 May 1902. Besides a small regiment of *Staatsartillerie* (110 guns), the Boers numbering 87,000 were mainly a part-time army of mounted horsemen. They were famous for their skilled marksmanship and could accurately hit a target at a distance of up to 1,000 yards. Thousands of foreigners volunteered from Europe to serve on the Boer side, and included a brigade of 300 local Irish led by Colonel John Young Filmore Blake, who later wrote a highly critical exposé of the British, *A West Pointer with the Boers*; as well as 50 American Irish from Chicago under Captain Patrick O'Connor who served as an ambulance unit. [55]

54 N. Ferguson, *The House of Rothschild, The World's Banker 1849-1999*, Vol. 2, Penguin Books, London, 1999, 416.
55 C. Nordbruch, *The European Volunteers of the Anglo-Boer War 1899-1902*, Contact Publishers, Pretoria, 1999, 141.

Members of the Transvaal Irish brigade led by Dr. John Filmore Blake.

On 31 October 1899 Winston Churchill arrived in Cape Town armed with 60 bottles of spirits and a supply of claret, as war correspondent for the *Morning Post* on a salary of £250 per month. In a great hurry to get to the action, on 15 November 1899 he commandeered an ammunition train travelling to Ladysmith in Natal, but near the town of Frere it was ambushed by a commando of Boers led by General Louis Botha. A large boulder had been placed at the bottom of a decline into which the steam engine crashed. Churchill was captured hiding under the train. As a journalist he had undertaken not to bear arms. However, a Mauser pistol containing lethal and illegal dum-dum bullets was found in his possession. On either of these counts the Boers would have been entitled to shoot him out of hand. If that had happened, the world could have been spared much future grief. He was then sent to a prisoner of war camp, the Staats Model School in Pretoria, where other captured British officers were held. One of his captors is reported to have said to Churchill, "You know it's those damned capitalists and Jews who have caused the war". [56] Churchill, whose mother Jennie Jerome was an American, tried to obtain relief from the United

---

56 R. Kraus, *op.cit.*, 98.

States Consulate, which was the protective power representing England. However, the consul, Charles E. Macrum, refused to help Churchill as he was "fanatically pro-Boer". [57] On 12 December 1899 Churchill escaped after climbing over a six foot boundary fence. He hid in a goods train under sacks of coal and reached Lourenço Marques, the capital of the then Portuguese colony of Mozambique, in rags and tatters nine days later.

Winston Churchill as a prisoner of war at a holding pen in Pretoria, November 1899. After his escape a reward of £25 was offered for his capture "dead or alive".

---

57 *Ibid.*, 98.

Initially, the Boers achieved some spectacular successes at Talana, Nicholson's Nek and Spioen Kop in Natal and at Magersfontein on the border of the Cape Colony and the Orange Free State, which was allied with the Transvaal Republic. However, the Boers adopted the wrong strategy. Instead of seizing the port of Durban and thereby preventing British reinforcements from landing, they conducted pointless sieges of Ladysmith, Kimberley and Mafeking. The duplicitous conduct of General Piet Joubert was responsible for this fiasco. He failed to advance to Durban, which he could have easily surrounded and thus prevented the landing of British troops.[58] In March 1900 he was found guilty of treason after a court martial in Pretoria and told to end his life with a revolver or take poison. He chose the poison on 28 March 1900. [59]

In November 1899 Smuts tried to meddle with the selection procedure of the Boer officer corps with a view to destabilising it. He proposed that the Boer officers should be elected by the burghers in a general election, which would have resulted in chaos.[60] While the Natal campaign was being fought Smuts took it upon himself to interfere with the command structure. He recommended that a weak commander, General Marthinus Prinsloo,[61] who was less informed of the conditions at the Tugela front, be placed in charge, instead of the far more reliable and experienced General Botha. Prinsloo's inadvertent appointment caused much dissension amongst the Boer High Command[62] and the Boers lost the initiative in Natal.

On 31 May 1900 Johannesburg fell to the overwhelming British forces. Prior to the city and its environs falling into British hands, Smuts had been entrusted by the Boer government with the wrecking of all the gold mines, but failed to execute this command and allowed the Acting Commandant, Dr. Krause, to arrest the leader of the saboteurs.[63]

---

58 H.R. Abercrombie, *op.cit.*, 238.
59 P.J. Pretorius, *op.cit.*, 65-66 and www.veritas.org.uk "Timeline of the Anglo-Boer War." Joubert's grave is a private Masonic temple.
60 P. C. Swanepoel , *op.cit.*, 69-70.
61 On 29 July 1900 General Prinsloo surrendered unconditionally to the British at Verliesfontein, now known as Surrender Hill, much to the disgust of the Freestaters.
62 P. C. Swanepoel , *op.cit.*, 71-73.
63 W.B. Worsfold, *op.cit.*, 145.

On 1 June 1900 a military council meeting of senior officers led by Botha and Smuts, who was acting transparently on behalf of the British, was held. It was decided to draft a telegram to President Krüger suggesting immediate surrender. [64] However, when President Steyn heard of this proposal he was furious and immediately intervened and rejected any notion of capitulation.

In the latter half of 1900 the powerful British Army of 448,725 failed to defeat the Boers on commando, of whom there were never more than 6,000 active at any one time, because they lacked the bush craft skills and tenacity of the Boers, who were fighting to defend their homeland. In contravention of the Hague Convention of 29 July 1899 with Respect to the Laws and Customs of War on Land, to which Convention Great Britain was a high contracting party, the British decided to wage war on women and children by means of a scorched earth policy. The Convention, which had come into force on 4 September 1900, bound Great Britain to observe its "rules of civilized warfare" in accordance with International Law. Instead homesteads,[65] as well as churches and public buildings, were burnt down, wells poisoned, cattle slaughtered (they were either burnt alive or had their hind legs cut and then left to die in order to save ammunition) and women were molested and raped. Over 155,000 women and children were herded into 48 concentration camps and housed in tents, even though temperatures in winter were often below zero. Not surprisingly 34,000 of them died, of whom 26,860 or 79% were under 16 years of age, from exposure, malnutrition and poor sanitation.[66]

Shortly before the British arrived in Pretoria in 4 June 1900, Smuts, on the orders of the Volksraad, withdrew the remaining £500,000 in gold and coin from the State Treasury and shipped it by train to the new capital in Middelburg,[67] as shells from the advancing British army landed near the railway station.[68]

---

64   T. Pakenham, *op.cit.*, 223.
65   90% of the homesteads in the Orange Free State were destroyed. "After the war vast expanses of land, which had belonged to prosperous Boer farmers, were bought for a song and redistributed to British soldiers". J.J. Peacock, *op.cit.*, 52.
66   For an in depth study of the concentration camps see S.M. Goodson, *The Rothschilds Role in the Genocide of the Boers*, *The Barnes Review*, Washington D.C., Vol. XXIII No.2, March/April 2017, 4-24.
67   P. C. Swanepoel , *op.cit.*, 74.
68   R.H. Kiernan, *General Smuts*, George G. Harrap & Company Ltd., London, 1944.

This £500,000 formed part of the "Krüger Millions" which only amounted to £1,250,000. Most of the balance of £750,000 was sent by the State Secretary, Dr. Willem Johannes Leyds aboard the German steamships *Bundelrath* and *Styria* to Europe.[69]

Battle of Nooitgedacht, Western Transvaal, where Jan Smuts deliberately allowed over 1,000 trapped British soldiers to escape. He was thereafter severely punished by General De la Rey for his incompetence and treachery.

After the British had captured Pretoria on 5 June 1900, Smuts took to the field in a military capacity. On 13 December 1900 at the battle of Nooitgedacht in the Magaliesberg, Smuts displayed inexplicable incompetence when he allowed two thirds of a British brigade, consisting of 1,500 troops and nine 4.7 inch naval guns under the command of Major General Ralph Clements, and which was trapped by 2,500 Boers in an indefensible position, to escape at Vaalkop. General de la Rey was so incensed with Smuts' ineptitude that he punished him with a thrashing with a sjambok.[70]

On 23 December 1900 Smuts sent a letter to General de la Rey in which he stated that the districts of Potchefstroom and Wolmaransstad were now under his command and that he would henceforth take on the military title of Acting Assistant Commandant General. In a postscript to another letter to De la Rey dated 16 February 1901, Smuts asked him to recommend to General Botha that his self-appointed rank be made official.[71]

---

69 H.R. Abercrombie, *op.cit.*, 78-79.
70 M. van Bart, Leeu van Wes-Transvaal verneder Jan Smuts oor pligsuim (The Lion of the Western Transvaal humiliates Jan Smuts on account of his dereliction of duty), *KultuurKroniek*, 10 February 2001. The severity of his punishment reinforces the probability that Smuts allowed the British to escape deliberately.
71 P. C. Swanepoel , *op.cit.*, 78-79 and S.G. Millin, *op.cit.*, 161.

John Bull: "Heavy? Of course it's heavy. But think of the glory."

In order to fund the Anglo-Boer War taxation skyrocketed, as increasing amounts of interest had to be paid to the Rothschild banks.

In May 1901 Smuts tried to initiate peace negotiations on behalf of his British masters. In June he travelled to Standerton, which coincidentally was under the command of Major General R.A.P. Clements, whom he had seemingly allowed to escape after the battle of Nooitgedacht six months previously. With the assistance of the Dutch Vice-Consul, De Heer A.D.R. Bisschop, a telegram was sent to President Krüger.[72] Krüger replied that surrender was out of the question and that the Boers must fight on, which was much to the disappointment of the British who were anxious to terminate this very costly war and the escalating amounts of interest which they were obliged to pay on the loans they owed to the Rothschilds and other associated banks.

---

72 *Ibid.*, 86-87.

While in Standerton Smuts was able to meet his wife Isie, who had not been confined to a concentration camp, as was the case with many of the wives of the Boer generals, but was living comfortably in a private home in Pietermaritzburg. At the same time Smuts held talks with General Clements, which may well have included instructions on how he was to conduct himself in the guerilla war in the Cape Colony. Instructions which presumably were that he should not instigate an uprising in the colony, but rather frustrate and prevent any such possibility .[73]

Compliments Card from the Rothschilds.
In December 1901 in order to boost the flagging morale of "their" troops, the three Rothschild brothers provided each soldier with a Christmas hamper containing sweets, some stationery, a portion of tobacco, a pipe, 12 packets of cigarettes, a book, a chocolate cake, a plum pudding and a pack of cards.

In August 1901 when Smuts set forth on his journey to the Cape instead of using a shorter route through Griqualand West and the Northern Cape, he travelled over a longer and more difficult route through the Orange Free State and north eastern Cape. A gap was left open at a disused ford, which Piet Swanepoel's research at the Pretoria archives has revealed, was pre-arranged at the instigation of Lord Herbert Kitchener.[74]

During his peregrinations in the Cape Colony, Smuts never discussed or consulted his men about his plans and remained silent. Commandant Piet Wessels became disillusioned with Smuts' leadership and after a month returned to the OFS with 100 of his men. Throughout his campaign there was only one engagement with the British at Modderfontein near Tarkastad

73   *Ibid.*, 88-89.
74   *Ibid.*, 99.

in the Eastern Cape on 17 September 1901.[75] Smuts played only a passive role and left the directing of the battle to his deputy, Commandant Ben Bouwer. When his forces were within fifty miles of Port Elizabeth , he refrained from making an attack.[76]

General Smuts with his horse "Charlie'. The Boer High Command instructed Smuts to foment a general uprising in the Cape Colony for which there was considerable scope and opportunity. Instead Smuts meandered around and achieved very little.

Smuts' orders from the Boer High Command had been to "foment a general uprising"[77] for which there was considerable support and sympathy. Instead as H.C. Armstrong writes in *Grey Steel* "All this marching seemed a waste. He had told them that the Cape Dutch would join them. They were not joining them. What was the use of it all?" [78] From the beginning Smuts had premeditatedly set out to sabotage his mission.

75   *Ibid.*, 115.
76   *Ibid.*, 113.
77   S.G. Millin, *op.cit.*, 161.
78   H.C. Armstrong, *op.cit.*, 117.

Towards the end of the war Swanepoel[79] highlights the anomalous circumstances regarding Smuts' brother-in-law, Tottie Krige acquiring a sack of gold, in order to finance the commando's operations, from Smuts' sick father residing in Malmesbury. Swanepoel's deduction is that this money "came from [British] Military Intelligence".[80]

At the end of April 1902 a Cape cart flying a large white flag tied to a pole above its canvas hood, approached Smuts with an offer of peace negotiations from Lord Kitchener, the commander-in-chief of the British forces. Smuts was given a safe conduct pass which enabled him to travel by troopship from Port Nolloth to Cape Town. He then boarded the battleship *HMS Monarch* in Simon's Town where he remained for a week and was treated "royally".[81]

---

79 P. C. Swanepoel , *op.cit.*, 116-12, Chapter 13 A Strange visit to borrow money.
80 *Ibid.*, 118.
81 *Ibid.*, 136.

Chapter IV

SURRENDER AND UNION

The commandos from the Orange Free State, including President Steyn and General Christiaan de Wet, also known as the *bittereinders*, were unanimous in their desire to fight on. With the summer rains, which would provide grazing and increased foliage for cover only four months away, they believed that the British would eventually capitulate from sheer exhaustion and from the heavy financial burden, which they were incurring.[82]

Smuts "in no uncertain terms crushed all hope that a general uprising of Afrikaners in the Cape would occur".[83] He was, however, contradicted by his deputy Barend Daniel Bouwer who found the situation quite different.

> "We now began to be much troubled by men desirous of joining us. Every day they arrived, complete with horse, saddle and bridle. Needing only a rifle and eager to take service. A very fine type they were too, it may be regrettable but it is a fact that the rebel always is. Ever since we arrived in the Colony we could have had a stream of recruits by merely saying the word; but in these parts – Clanwilliam, Piketberg, Vanrhynsdorp – they were more persistent than anywhere else."[84]

Smuts was only the legal adviser of the Transvaal delegation, but it seems that he was present on Kitchener's insistence.[85] He prevailed upon the 60 delegates (30 from each republic) to surrender and to accept the British terms without delay. Peace was signed at the Treaty of Vereeniging on 31 May 1902, after 54 of the 60 Boer delegates had voted in favour of acceptance of the terms of the treaty. When Smuts informed his commando of the peace terms, the voice of Commandant Japie Neser shouted out: *"Jan*

---

82   T. Pakenham, *op.cit.*, 561.
83   L. Scholtz, *Why the Boers Lost the War*, Palgrave Macmillan, London, 2005, 320.
84   B.P. Bouwer, *Memoirs of General Bouwer*, Human Sciences Research Council, Pretoria, 1980, 215.
85   P. C. Swanepoel , *op.cit.*, 137.

Smuts, jy het ons verraai!" (Jan Smuts, you have betrayed us!).[86] 72% of the Transvaal population of 288,750 had either perished or been taken prisoner.[87] The British government paid out compensation to the Boers of £3 million, but this was a derisory amount in relation to the destruction and loss of life caused.

In 1903 Joseph Chamberlain visited the former republics. In order to repair and run the newly acquired colonies, he raised a loan, which was underwritten by the Rothschilds, who have always specialised in this type of finance, whereby money is created out of thin air and then lent at interest. This loan of £35 million[88] was issued at 3% per annum and was guaranteed by the Imperial Government.[89]

On 9 November 1905 on the birthday of King Edward VII, the fabulous Cullinan diamond weighing 3,106.7 carats or 621.35g was donated to the British Crown "as a token of Boer loyalty"[90] and "as a thank offering for responsible government".[91] Smuts was instrumental in donating the diamond, but rather as an expression of gratitude for a further loan of £5 million which the Rothschilds had lent to the colony.

On 5 December 1905 there was a change of government in England when the Conservatives resigned and the leader of the Liberal Party, Sir Henry Campbell-Bannerman, became prime minister. Smuts travelled to England and on 26 January 1906 he had a constructive interview with Winston Churchill, who was the Under-Secretary of State for the Colonies. Campbell-Bannerman, was also sympathetic to the cause of the Boers. However, it should be noted that Churchill was the driving force and made the announcement of the terms for self-government in the House of Commons on 31 July 1906.[92]

---

86 P.J. Pretorius, *op.cit.*, 64 as quoted in D. Harrison, *The White Tribe of Africa: South Africa in Perspective*, Johannesburg, Southern Book Publishers, 1987, 45 and P. Meiring, *Smuts the Patriot*,Tafelberg Publishers, 1975, 52. In addition Smuts did not contest the draconian provision which did not grant the Cape Rebels amnesty and thereby condemned them to long terms of imprisonment and stiff fines, *Songs of the Veld*, Introduced by M. van Bart, Cederberg Publishers, Kenilworth, South Africa, 2008, lxxxv. First published by New Age Press, 1902.
87 J.J. Peacock, *op.cit.*, 46.
88 £3.9 billion in 2016 values.
89 S.G. Millin, *op.cit.*, 202.
90 *Ibid.*, 229.
91 *Ibid.*, 257.
92 J.W. Muller, *Churchill as Peacemaker*, Woodrow Wilson Center Series and Cambridge University Press, 1997, 139, 142.

On 20 February 1907, elections for responsible government for the Transvaal were held. The party of *Het Volk* (The People), which was founded on 23 May 1904, was led by General Louis Botha (1862-1919), a freemason. During the election held on 20 February 1907, Smuts repudiated a *Het Volk* candidate who advocated restricting Jewish immigration, stating that: "The Russian Jews who come to this country intend to make it their home; they always have been, and will continue to be, welcomed by our organisation. No measures are ever likely to be taken to restrict their immigration to this country." [93] The party won 37 or 53.6% of the 69 seats.

Smuts was appointed colonial secretary and minister of education, but made himself unpopular by making the English language the medium of instruction from Standard IV onwards. After the announcement of the cabinet, an English cartoonist, Arthur Wynell Lloyd, later of *Punch* magazine, illustrated a *Het Volk* cabinet meeting consisting of six ministers all with the face of Smuts. The description read: "The controlling influence of General Smuts in the Cabinet is so apparent that the Government may be said to be concentrated in him alone." [94] Although Louis Botha was the ostensible head of the government, he was a weak and ignorant man[95] and Smuts was the real power wielder.

From 1906 Smuts had to contend with ever-increasing immigration of Indians into the Transvaal. (They were not permitted to live in the Orange Free State). Protests against an Act compelling all Indians to register, were led by an attorney from Durban, Mahatma Gandhi, who resided in South Africa from 1893-1914.

93 S.G. Millin, *op.cit.*, 223-224. Between 1880 and 1910 the Jewish population increased from 4,000 to 40,000 with the addition of 36,000 mainly Yiddish speaking Lithuanians. Some of the first of these immigrants arrived in 1885 on the *SS Peru*. They were notorious for their dishonest and unscrupulous behaviour, and even now anyone who engages in such a fraudulent manner in the Jewish community is said to be pulling off a "Peruvian trick". Later some of the descendants of these Jews would play a prominent role in the overthrow and ruination of civilised government in South Africa through their support of the South African Communist Party and the African National Congress. In *Cutting Through The Mountain*, edited by I. Suttner, Viking Penguin, Johannesburg, 1997, it is revealed that almost half of the 27 South African Jewish activists interviewed, claimed Lithuanian ancestry.
94 *Ibid.*, 228.
95 Maria Elizabeth Rothman in *My Beskeie Deel – 'n Outobiografiese Vertelling*, Tafelberg, Kaapstad, 1972, mentions a conversation which she had with General JBM Hertzog who said that *"Louis Botha het twee dingle teen hom: swakheid en onkunde ... Botha het'n besef van beginsel, maar kan dit nie handhaaf nie."* (Louis Botha has two things against him: weakness and ignorance ...Botha has an awareness of principle, but is unable to maintain it), as cited in J.A. Marais, *Die era van Verwoerd*, Aktuele Publikasies, Pretoria, 1992, 218.

Gandhi, who advocated *Satyagraha* (a Sanskrit word meaning devotion to the truth), adopted passive resistance tactics, which would be used to great effect in India in the 1920s and 1930s. Smuts would, however, not relent and Gandhi had to spend a year in jail.

General Louis Botha was Commander-in-Chief (1900-1902) of the Transvaal Boers. During his premiership (1910-1919), he left the political affairs of state almost entirely in the hands of Smuts.

Smuts then worked actively to unify the two British colonies of the Cape and Natal and the two former Boer republics of Orange Free State and Transvaal into one nation. He was responsible for doing most of the research and drafting of a constitution, which had a unitary form rather than a federal one. A successful National Convention was held in the Durban Town Hall from October 1908 to May 1909 and the Union of South Africa came into existence on 31 May 1910.

The controversial Louis Botha was elected prime minister of the new Union of South Africa, but the real power behind the scenes continued to be Jannie Smuts, who held the cabinet portfolios of interior, defence and later finance. In 1912 the British made Botha an honorary general of the British Army and a Privy Councillor. He had also adopted the fashion of wearing knee breeches, silk stockings and court dress since the Imperial Conference held in May 1911. This behaviour was viewed as symbolic of national treason and deeply offended many of the Boer people. [96]

On 23 February 1912 Smuts introduced a bill for a Defence Force Act, which included proposals for a Defence Force Council and the establishment of a military college for the training of officers. The bill was vigorously opposed by former Boer general, Christiaan Beyers, not only as regards to the structure of the Union Defence Force, but to the fact that it could be deployed in service of the British Empire anywhere in the world. [97] The bill was adopted on 13 June 1912.

Many of the Boers, particularly in the Orange Free State, still felt that they had been sold out to the British. In November 1913 General Hertzog (a grandson of a German immigrant) was forced out of the cabinet after a reshuffle and left the ruling South African Party together with five other party members. On 2 July 1914 he formed the National Party.

96   J.J. McCord, *op.cit.*, 273.
97   L. J. Bothma, *Rebelspoor*, Self-published, Langenhovenpark, Orange Free State, 2015, 129-131.

Chapter V

WORLD WAR I, THE 1914 REBELLION, GERMAN SOUTH WEST AFRICA AND GERMAN EAST AFRICA

In January 1914 a railway strike began as a result of workers having been laid off after the amalgamation of the four colonial railways. This was followed by a miners' strike, in which Smuts ordered police to use force and 21 miners were subsequently shot dead. He then deported the nine leaders of the strike on the *SS Umgeni* without due legal process having taken place, and without having obtained the consent of the cabinet and parliament. Smuts then forced through parliament an Act of Indemnity which protected him from prosecution.

In July 1914, World War I broke out after the heir to the Austrian throne, Archduke Franz Ferdinand, and his Czech-born wife were assassinated in Sarajevo, Bosnia Herzegovina. The crime was committed by Gavrilo Princeps, allegedly a Jew, who was a member of the Black Hand, a Rothschild front, and an associate of Leon Trotsky (real name Lev Davidovitsj Bronstein).

The invasion of German South West Africa, considered by many Boers, who now called themselves Afrikaners, to be a friendly nation, was the catalyst which precipitated the rebellion. It was started on 9 October 1914 by former Boer War general, Manie Maritz, who was joined a few weeks later by Generals Christiaan Beyers and Christiaan de Wet. They were supported by 11,400 rebels. However, without the inspirational leadership of Koos de la Rey, who had been expected to play a decisive role, but had been accidentally killed at a road block on 15 September 1914, it quickly petered out. It lost momentum when General de Wet was captured on 1 December 1914 and General Beyers drowned on 8 December 2014, while trying to escape across the Vaal river and came to an end on 30 January 1915. Most of the rebel leaders were treated leniently and the rebels were sent home on parole. The exception was Commandant Jopie Fourie, who because he had joined the rebellion as a defence force member, was sentenced to death by a military tribunal. Dr. Daniel Malan and a delegation of five prominent persons tried to intercede, but when they arrived at Smuts' farm, *Doornkloof*, near Irene 15 miles (25 km) south of Pretoria, Smuts slipped away in a craven manner and spent the night at the Pretoria Club where they were unable to find him. A prison sentence would have been more appropriate, but Smuts, who was minister of defence refused to grant a reprieve and this ruthlessness of his only served to increase his unpopularity amongst conservative Afrikaners.[98]

General Victor Franke commander of the *schutztruppe* in German South West Africa.

On 10 September 1914 the House of Assembly voted by 91 to 12 votes[99] to accede to Great Britain's request that South Africa invade German South West Africa, notwithstanding the considerable opposition of many Boers who sympathized with Germany – a country which did not pose any threat towards South Africa. In February 1915 an expeditionary force of 67,000, mainly volunteer soldiers, under General Louis Botha invaded German South West Africa (now Namibia). They were opposed by 3,000 *schutztruppe* (protection force) commanded by Colonel Joachim von Heydebreck, who after his death on 12 November 1914 was succeeded by Major Victor Franke. The ostensible

98 *Ibid.*, 356-364.
99 L. J. Bothma, *op.cit.*, 165.

motive of the expeditionary force was to seize the powerful wireless transmitters at Lüderitzbucht and Swakopmund, which it was alleged would be used for transmitting messages to the German High Seas Fleet. However, the real aim was to secure the diamond fields on the southern coast for Ernest Oppenheimer,[100] the Rothschilds' representative in South Africa and who was also mayor of Kimberley. These diamond fields, and in particular near the *Koloniale Bergbaugesellschaft* founded by August Stauch, were responsible for 21% of world production at that time, and their capture would enable De Beers Consolidated Mines to obtain a monopoly and fix the prices of diamonds in their favour. Together with their militia, the Germans could only muster a combined force of 10,000 men with which to defend their immense territory of 318,262 square miles (823,616 square kilometers), and within a year they were defeated. The surrender took place at the *Alte Feste* (Old Fort) in Windhoek on 9 July 1915. 103 German and 269 South African soldiers lost their lives in this pointless campaign. It may thus be observed that the South African troops who took part in this military adventure were not fighting for King and Country, but for Rothschild and Oppenheimer.

At the Conference of Berlin (15 November 1884 – 26 February 1885) Great Britain was one of 13 European nations which signed the Congo Act. This declaration stipulated that in the event of a European war, the colonies in the basin of the Congo would remain neutral. However, on 5 August 1914 British troops from the Uganda protectorate violated the agreement and commenced hostilities by attacking German outposts near Lake Victoria.

Smuts had played only a minor role in the conquest of South West Africa and was envious of Botha's success; thus when the offer came in February 1916 to take command of the campaign in German East Africa (Tanganyika, now Tanzania), he accepted with alacrity.

---

100   L. J. Bothma, *op.cit.*, 403, 410-411. The Kimberley Regiment played an important role in securing the diamond fields and when they returned on 9 August 1915, "...the De Beers hooters were blown as part of the official reception and speeches of welcome were made by the mayor [Ernest Oppenheimer] and others". H.H. Curson, *The History of the Kimberley Regiment*, Northern Cape Printers, Kimberley, 1963, 158 and 161.

General von Lettow-Vorbeck, commander of the German forces in East Africa and Smuts at a dinner in London in early December 1929.

Smuts was appointed a lieutenant-general, but failed to come to grips with the logistics required for the conquest of such a vast tropical territory. Heavy rains, lack of food, the unhealthy climate and disease, principally malaria, which also affected Smuts, prevented him from defeating the Germans. A force of 600 Germans and 6,000 Askaris under the command of the intrepid General Paul Emil von Lettow-Vorbeck[101] outwitted Smuts and his army of 93,300. When he embarked from Dar-es-Salaam, 400 of his officers awaiting repatriation refused to give him a farewell parade. Von Lettow-Vorbeck only surrendered two weeks after the end of the war on 25 November 1918. Smuts only had experience in guerilla warfare and his abilities in a more conventional war under different conditions were severely exposed.

---

101   J.C. Smuts (Jnr.), *Jan Christian Smuts*, Cassell & Company Ltd, Cape Town, 1952. After World War II Smuts sent Von Lettow-Vorbeck food parcels, which were presumably much appreciated.

Chapter VI

SMUTS IN BRITAIN, BALFOUR DECLARATION, VERSAILLES, LEAGUE OF NATIONS AND IRELAND

In March 1917 Smuts joined the Imperial War Cabinet at the invitation of Prime Minister Lloyd George. He also became a member of the Privy Council. He was received with a "whirlwind of applause" [102] in Great Britain. In May 1917 Smuts was offered command of the British forces fighting the Turks in the Middle East, but Botha wisely advised him to turn the offer down.

On 18 May 1917 at a banquet held in his honour in the Royal Gallery of the House of Lords, Smuts said that the British Empire denoted a single entity, consisting of many nations, states and colonies and protectorates and should in future therefore be designated the British Commonwealth of Nations, which term eventually passed into common use. [103]

On 7 July 1917 after twenty-two German Gotha aeroplanes, bombed London, destroying a large number of buildings and causing huge fires, there was a great public outcry. Smuts was chosen to settle this problem and within eight days he completed a scheme, which was based on a centralized command structure for the defence of London. Shortly thereafter Smuts produced a report, which the British cabinet described as "the most important paper in the history of the creation of the Royal Air Force". [104] Smuts proposed the formation of an Air Ministry, which would amalgamate the Royal Flying Corps and the Royal Naval Air Service". [105] He was also appointed Chairman of the War Priorities Committee, which settled priority claims among departments concerned with the war and allocated manpower resources.

---

102   H.C. Armstrong, *op.cit.*, 276.
103   R.H. Kiernan, *op.cit.*, 90-91.
104   *Ibid.*, 104.
105   *Ibid.*, 105.

During his time in England Smuts gave many patriotic speeches, one of which prevented a coalminers' strike in Tonypandy, south-east Wales, which was threatening to cripple Britain's war effort. Lloyd George had tipped off Smuts before he went to Wales, that the Welsh were great singers. Before he addressed the tens of thousands of strikers on 29 October 1917, Smuts asked them to sing the Welsh national anthem *Land of my Fathers*. In this manner he was able to diffuse a very volatile situation and the strike was called off.[106]

On 2 November 1917, together with Lord Arthur Balfour, Smuts drew up the infamous Balfour Declaration[107] after it had gone through five drafts. This document promised Palestine, which was part of the Ottoman Empire at that time, to the Jews in an effort to gain the support of American Jewry, who had been instrumental in forcing President Woodrow Wilson (himself a victim of Jewish blackmail)[108] to declare war on Germany on 6 April 1917.

Smuts also took part in two exploratory diplomatic missions. The first one involved preliminary talks in December 1917 in Geneva with the Jewish Austrian ambassador, Count Albert von Mensdorff, who represented the Foreign Minister of Austria, Ottkar von Czernin, about concluding a separate peace with the Austro-Hungarian Empire. However, von Mensdorff was only interested in acting as a mediator, who would bring Germany into discussions about peace terms. Thus no agreement was reached.[109] The other mission took place in April 1919 during the Versailles peace conference, when he met the revolutionary leader of Hungary, Bela Kun (real name Aaron Cohen) at Budapest railway station with a view to using him as a vehicle for communicating with Moscow and persuading Russia to attend the peace conference and to bring about a cessation of hostilities between Hungary and Romania.[110] The latter mission also did not achieve any success.

---

106   *Ibid.*, 293-5.
107   J.C. Smuts (Jnr.), *op.cit.*, 204.
108   M.C. Piper, The Making of Woodrow Wilson – An American Nero?, *The Barnes Review*, Washington D.C., Vol. VI, No. 2. March/April 2000, 6-12.
109   R.H. Kiernan, *op.cit.*, 96-99.
110   *Ibid.*, 114.

At the end of 1918 Smuts resigned from the Imperial War Cabinet, even though King George V had privately asked him "to stay on and become Prime Minister".[111]

After Germany had been induced to sign an armistice on 11 November 1918, based on the Fourteen Points of Woodrow Wilson, a peace conference was held at the Palace of Versailles in Paris. Before it had even commenced, it was declared in the press that Germany was solely responsible for the war, in spite of the fact that Germany did not plot a European war, did not want one and had made genuine efforts to avert one. The conference was "poisoned by British perfidy and French hatred and ignorance"[112] and the 14 Points were ignored. As Smuts would later admit, "Everything we have done here is far worse than the Congress of Vienna.[113] The statesmen of 1815 at least knew what was going on. Our statesmen had no idea."[114]

An explanation for this ignorance of the Allied leaders may be found in the fact that they were all assisted by Jewish advisers, who were manipulating the conference to suit their own clandestine purposes and in particular the cause of Zionism. According to Benjamin H. Freedman, who attended the conference, there were 117 Jews present.[115] The advisers of Lloyd George and Georges Clemenceau were Sir Philip Sassoon (mother née de Rothschild) and Georges Mandel (real name Jeroboam Rothschild) respectively. Woodrow Wilson was assisted by the Jews Bernard Baruch and Louis Brandeis. The Italian delegate Baron Sidney Sonino was half-Jewish, while the interpreter Etienne Mantoux and the military adviser Mr. Kish were also Jews.

---

111   P. Beukes, *op.cit.*, 186.
112   L. Degrelle, *Hitler Born At Versailles*, Vol. 1 of The Hitler Century, Institute for Historical Review, Costa Mesa, California, 1987, 335.
113   The Congress of Vienna was a conference of ambassadors of European states chaired by Prince Klemens von Metternich. It was held from September 1814 to June 1815 and settled the issues arising from the French Revolutionary Wars, the Napoleonic Wars and the dissolution of the Holy Roman Empire.
114   L. Degrelle, *op.cit.*, 361.
115   Speech given at the Willard Hotel, Washington in 1961. https://www.youtube.com/watch?v=aHdXiRKjwJI

Smuts attended Versailles with Botha as the South African representatives and made his presence known by writing a memorandum *The League of Nations – A Practical Suggestion.*[116] In a letter to his wife dated 15 January 1919, Smuts informed his wife that his "pamphlet has made a great impression in high circles, and not least on President Wilson". It formed the basis for the *Covenant of the League of Nations* and was accepted by Woodrow Wilson, who frequently consulted Smuts when in need of advice.[117]

To his credit Smuts realized that the swingeing financial burdens which France proposed to place on Germany would be incapable of being effected and would sow the seeds of future conflict. He encouraged John Maynard Keynes, who was also attending and had calculated that Germany would be unable to make reparations on the scale envisaged, to write *The Economic Consequences of the Peace.*[118] Although Smuts protested strenuously against the so called "punishment clauses", [119] it is ironic that he proposed the most draconian impost of all viz. the payment of pensions and separation allowances to the victors, which would have exceeded all the other nine categories of reparations.[120] It was rejected. On 28 June 1919 the German delegation was forced to sign the treaty in the face of a naval blockade imposed by the British navy, which was intent on starving the Germans into submission.

Initially, Smuts refused to sign the treaty, but Lloyd George persuaded him to sign and then protest afterwards. Smuts was, however, being a little disingenuous, because if he had not signed, he might have jeopardized the granting of South West Africa to South Africa as a Class C mandate, which gave South Africa full powers of legislation and administration over the territory as an integral part of the Union of South Africa. The exercise of these powers was vested by the House of Assembly in the governor-general (Union Act No. 49 of 1919), who later delegated them to the administrator of South West Africa.

Between 20 June and 5 August 1921 Smuts attended an Imperial Conference in London. During his stay there Smuts travelled to

---

116   P. Beukes, *op.cit.*, 175.
117   H.C. Armstrong, *op.cit.*, 321-3.
118   J.C. Smuts (Jnr.), *op.cit.*, 222.
119   P. Beukes, *op.cit.*, 177.
120   C. Quigley, *op.cit.*, 326.

In June 1920 Smuts met Irish leader, Éamon de Valera, and persuaded him to cease hostilities and accept political status as a British dominion.

Ireland, incognito,[121] in an effort to quell the rebellion there. Éamon de Valera, the Irish leader, refused to meet the Ulster leader, James Craig, but was prepared to meet the Boer, Smuts. Smuts met Arthur Griffith,[122] de Valera and Erskine Childers and persuaded them to cease hostilities, attend a conference and accept dominion status. On the advice of Smuts, King George V gave a conciliatory speech at the opening of the parliament in Belfast on 21 June 1921. A truce followed on 11 July 1921 and after protracted negotiations an agreement was reached, which resulted in the signing of the Anglo-Irish Treaty on 6 December 1921.[123] Exactly one year later the Irish Free State was proclaimed.

---

121   He used the nom-de-plume Mr. Smith.
122   Smuts knew Griffith while he had been a journalist in Johannesburg before the Anglo-Boer War.
123   R.H. Kiernan, *op.cit.*, 127.

Chapter VII

SMUTS INTRODUCES CENTRAL BANK AND INCOME TAX

Louis Botha died on 27 August 1919 and Smuts was appointed prime minister, an office he would occupy until his electoral defeat on 19 June 1924. Botha, who had been in poor health for some time was suffering from the Spanish influenza. Overcome with guilt on account of his treasonous behaviour at the peace negotiations in May 1902 after the end of the Anglo-Boer War, when he meekly capitulated, Botha reportedly slashed his wrists in order to hasten his end. [124]

It was during this period that Smuts committed the most foolish blunder of his entire political career. This was the establishment of a central bank known as the South African Reserve Bank. It was enacted by means of the Banking and Currency Act, which was very similar to the Banking and Currency Act of the United States of America, which Congress had been misled into approving on 23 December 1913 and which brought into existence the 58% Rothschild owned US Federal Reserve Bank. This treacherous piece of legislation would enable the seigniorage benefits of creating money out of nothing to be transferred to the private banks in perpetuity.[125] This form of debt slavery would later ensure that the most productive sector of the population, namely the Whites, would dwindle from 25% of the population at that time to the present day 8%. Usury is one of the principal causes of the impoverishment of the nuclear family, decline in the birth rate and collapse in civilisation; a consequence, which Oswald Spengler highlighted in his *The Decline of the West*. [126]

---

124   P.J. Pretorius, *op.cit.*, 66.
125   Lionel Rothschild, the grandson of the founder of the Rothschild dynasty, Mayer Amschel Rothschild (1714-1812), once said to Disraeli "Can anything be more absurd than that a nation should apply to an individual to maintain its credit, its existence as a state and its comfort as a people".
126   O. Spengler, *The Decline of the West*, Alfred A. Knopf, Inc., Munich, 1926, 250-251. K. Bolton, *Knut Hamsun*, Renaissance Press, Paraparaumu Beach, New Zealand, 6-7 and on page 9 discusses "...since Hamsun's time the spiraling spiritual impoverishment and the alienation that has been wrought by the primacy of the city and of money over the land and culture that had been expressed on a philosophical level by Spengler.

Sir Henry Strakosch, who connived with Smuts in the establishment of the
South African Reserve Bank and the subsequent enslavement of the people of
South Africa through debt and usury.

Previously, Smuts had been appointed minister of finance in 1912,
even though he "had never shown any financial ability......had
no experience of business......his personal finances and his
accounts were haphazard and usually neglected......he was
useless at all detail". [127] In 1914 he piloted through the Income
Tax Act, shortly after the United States had enacted its own
Income Tax Act in 1913. (This is the so called 16th Amendment,
which was not approved by a majority of states). There was
much laughter in the house[128] when Smuts' bill was first
introduced. The tax threshold was set at £1,000, equivalent to
the annual salary of a high earning executive and the act itself
was subject to annual review as to its retention. The threshold
was quickly lowered and the review was soon forgotten. Income
tax forms an integral part of the usury system, enabling the
payment of interest on government loans, which private
bankers have created out of nothing. In 1915 Smuts was
relieved of his post. Piet Beukes comments that his period of
office as "Minister of Finance proved to be a mistake", [129]
while his opponents called him "an indifferent and casual
administrator". [130]

127 H.C. Armstrong, *op.cit.*, 253, 272.
128 *The Cape Times,* 24 April 1914.
129 P. Beukes, *op.cit.*, 147.
130 S.G. Millin, *op.cit.*, 262.

The Banking and Currency Act of 1920 had to do with the stabilisation of the country's gold reserves and the minting and printing of South Africa's own coin and bank notes respectively. However, its principal objective was the establishment of a central bank. Smuts asked a friend of his, Sir Henry Strakosch, who was a retired mining magnate living in England to provide guidance. Strakosch was a Moravian Jew who in later life, like Ernest Oppenheimer and Benjamin Disraeli,[131] had converted to Anglicanism (Episcopalianism). Strakosch wrote a pamphlet titled *The South African Currency and Exchange Problem* and this memorandum was used as a basis for the legislation.

First South African Reserve Bank building, 30 June 1921

The bill was strongly opposed by the Labour Party, with one of its members Frank Nettleton saying: "The banks have been the factor in the enslavement of the workers, and as they merely exist to loan great enterprises at exorbitant interest, they must be inimical to the good of the people as a whole. It is time Ministers of Finance all over the world consider the establishment of state banks…What asses we were to allow our wealth to get into the hands of private banks, instead of having a state bank of our own". [132] The bill was passed by 69 votes to 22. Shortly thereafter Strakosch set off for India to establish the Reserve Bank of India.

---

131   Disraeli converted to Anglicanism at the age of 12.
132   *The Cape Times*, 17 July 1920.

In the 1930s, while Winston Churchill was out of office and quite often spent time in sanatoriums recovering from alchoholic binges, he ran into financial difficulties because of his gambling debts and after his stock exchange investments had failed. On 26 March 1936, he had one week in which to settle his debts or lose his treasured home Chartwell in Kent.[133] Strakosch stepped into the breach and paid Churchill's debts. Churchill's tone changed dramatically thereafter from being frank and independent, as he was in the 1920s, to one of servility towards "other interests". Strakosch would feed Churchill with exaggerated and often spurious statistics regarding German rearmament in order to promote a war psychosis.[134] Churchill became a vehement enemy of Germany, which had abandoned the exploitative usury system and reconstituted the Reichsbank as a state bank serving the needs of all Germany's people.

Strakosch died in London on 30 October 1943 and in his will dated 27 August 1941 he expunged Churchill's debt of £18,162.[135] He also left a further £20,000 to Churchill and £10,000[136] to Smuts, stating in the case of the latter bequest that it was "as a token of friendship and gratitude reposed in me in connection with the several tasks he has entrusted to me". [137] These were the only major bequests. In such a manner are "friends" rewarded for past services rendered.[138]

133   D. Irving, *Churchill's War, The Struggle for Power*, Veritas Publishing Company Pty Ltd, Bullsbrook, Western Australia, 1987, 104.

134   W.S. Churchill, *The Second World War, The Gathering Storm*, Vol. I, Cassell & Co. Ltd, London, 1948, 193 and D. Irving, *op.cit.*, 49.

135   Last Will and Testament of Sir Henry Strakosch, 10.

136   The Bank of England's Inflation Calculator http://www.bankofengland.co.uk/education/inflation/indexhtm £18,162 were worth £1,177,919, £20,000 were worth £836,854 and £10,000 were worth £418,427 respectively in 2016.

137   Last Will, *op.cit.*, 7-8.

138   Ten years after the Anglo-Boer War in 1912 Smuts had become a very rich man and owned 10 farms aggregating over 50,000 acres. W.K. Hancock, *Smuts, Vol. 1: The Sanguine Years, 1870-1919,* Cambridge University Press, 1962, 168. In similar fashion ex-President F.W. de Klerk, who also had not made a success of his legal practice, became fabulously wealthy after he sold South Africa out to the international bankers in the early 1990s. In 2010 it was revealed that De Klerk had over one billion Swiss francs (R13.75 billion) stashed away in a secret bank account in Liechtenstein. S.M. Goodson, *Inside the South African Reserve Bank Its Origins and Secrets Exposed*, Black House Publishing Ltd, London, 2014, 14-15.

Striking mineworkers being machine gunned in central Johannesburg. Smuts sided with the Chamber of Mines (the mine owners) and employed brutal force in order to suppress white miners, who were protesting against their replacement by lowly paid black mineworkers.

To return to South Africa, in 1921 there was an economic downturn with a consequent rise in unemployment. The mine owners represented by South Africa's Chamber of Mines decided to cut costs by employing more Black miners at £3 a month at the expense of the White miners, who were being paid £30 a month. The main trade union, the Industrial Federation, which was under the influence of Bolshevik agitators, demanded control of the mines. Negotiations failed and were followed by a violent strike by over 20,000 miners in January 1922. Smuts, who was figuratively speaking in the pocket of the mining magnates,[139] after an initial period of inactivity on the government's part, decided not to intervene, but to crush the strike by using force. The defence force was called up and the strike was brutally suppressed by means of aircraft, artillery and machine guns. Almost 5,000 people were arrested, 1,400 strikers were prosecuted, 864 were convicted on charges of high treason, hundreds were sentenced to long terms of imprisonment, 18 were condemned to death and four were hanged. 535 Whites and 152 Blacks lost their lives in the uprising. A few months later on 22 May 1922 Smuts employed identical methods when suppressing an uprising – apparently over the zealous implementation of a dog tax - of the Nama tribe at Hakkiesdoorn along the Orange River in South West Africa. [140]

Smuts' high-handed and merciless treatment of the strikers made him deeply unpopular, and it came as no surprise when his party, the South African Party, which had merged with the Unionist Party under Sir Thomas Smartt in November 1920, lost the general election on 19 June 1924. General Hertzog's National Party obtained 63 seats and together with the Labour Party's 18 seats formed a coalition.

In 1925 Smuts played the leading role in arranging the Locarno Treaty which was signed in London on 1 December 1925. This treaty consisted of nine pacts between Germany, Belgium, Czechoslovakia, France and Poland. The principal one was the Rhine Pact which guaranteed the frontier between Germany and Belgium - France against attack from either side and was also signed by Britain and Italy.

---

139   According to the General Smuts Foundation, the preservation of Smuts' house
        was enabled with the assistance of "generous donations from the mining houses".
140   L.J. Bothma L.J., *op.cit.*, 411.

In 1926 Smuts completed his major work, which was originally drafted as *An Inquiry into the Whole*, but was published as *Holism and Evolution*[141]. It expanded on his theory that by combining small parts one creates a whole larger than the individual parts. He applied this theory to practical effect in uniting the four colonies into South Africa and it was his desire that southern and central Africa become a dominion under South African rule. The British Commonwealth was a further extension of that concept and a new world order under a world government was projected to be the logical, final outcome, with the qualification that Smuts' holism was restricted to the white race only.

General JBM Hertzog, Prime Minister (1924-1939), who did all in his powers to prevent South Africa from embarking on a fratricidal war in September 1939.

In 1926 General Hertzog attended the Imperial Conference in London and declared his intention of seeking independence for the dominions. Smuts opposed this intention and declared at the Johannesburg City Hall on 20 August 1926, "Everybody knows that any such declaration will mean the disintegration of the Empire" (*Volkstem*). Two months later at Pietersburg on 25 October 1926, Smuts said that "We are satisfied with the British Empire. We are satisfied with the position" (*Rand Daily Mail*).[142]

---

141   Holism is pronounced Hollism.
142   J.J. McCord, *op.cit.*, 473.

For the next nine years Smuts would remain as leader of the opposition in parliament, but his high profile days were in abeyance. He was now able to devote more time to his farming activities, mountaineering and his favourite hobby, botany, and in particular the study of grasses. Smuts was one of the world's leading experts on savannah grass and could name and identify every species of grass in South Africa. One type of fingergrass, *Digitaria smutsii* , has been named in his honour, although it later transpired that it had already been described as *Digitaria eriantha.*

He still travelled abroad, mainly to England, where he frequently gave speeches. Whenever he made such trips, his opponents in South Africa would sarcastically remark that he was going "home". In his speeches he would often refer to a "new world order". As previously mentioned he was also responsible for proposing that the British Empire be called the British Commonwealth of Nations.[143] In 1930 Smuts wrote a book *Africa and Some World Problems* and became a Fellow of the Royal Society. In 1931 Smuts became the first president of the British Association for the Advancement of Science, who was not from Great Britain. His address was titled "The Scientific World Picture Today" and his contribution mentioned new developments in physics, nuclear physics and astronomical theory. From 1931-1934 he was Rector of Scotland's oldest university St Andrews and from 1948-1950 Chancellor of Cambridge University.

In the early 1930s the Great Depression, which had been engineered by the Jewish-owned and -controlled US Federal Reserve Bank,[144] principally by the withdrawal of credit, gathered momentum. South Africa had unwisely remained on the gold standard after its main trading partner England had already left it on 19 September 1931, and this served to exacerbate the economic slump. Meanwhile the South African Reserve Bank lost half of its capital and all of its reserves and teetered on the brink of bankruptcy. South Africa finally withdrew from the gold standard on 27 December 1932.

After the general election of 17 May 1933, General Hertzog proposed that in view of the economic crisis the two main parties, the National and South African parties merge into the United Party and rule the country jointly. Smuts agreed and accepted the posts of deputy prime minister and minister of justice.

143   H.C. Armstrong, *op.cit.*, 285.
144   Three of the five US Federal Reserve Board governors were Jewish in November 2010. Three years earlier all five Board members were Jewish.

Chapter VIII

SMUTS THE WARMONGER

On 30 January 1933 the National Socialists came to power in Germany. Instead of apprising himself of what this new movement portended, Smuts confined himself to making contemptuous and jejune remarks, such as that national socialism was a "dark force that threatened freedom" [145] and was a form of enslavement.[146] In April 1937 he described Germany's Four Year Plan as a "colossal mistake from an economic point of view", [147] notwithstanding the fact that her GDP was growing at 10% per annum and there was almost zero unemployment, while on 30 June 1938 he bizarrely went on to claim that Germany was "in a very bad way economically and financially". [148]

Smuts' minister of defence, Oswald Pirow (1890-1959), a son of German immigrants ,[149] had visited Adolf Hitler in 1933 and 1938,[150] and thus Smuts had been kept informed of the impressive economic and social transformation[151] which had taken place in that country. Between 1933 and 1939 Germany's Gross Domestic Product doubled, while South Africa was still wallowing in recession. According to the Carnegie Commission of Investigation on the Poor White Question in South Africa published in 1932, one third of the Afrikaners were living as paupers.

---

145   J.C. Smuts (Jnr.), *op.cit.*, 348.
146   P. Beukes, *op.cit.*, 126.
147   P.B. Blanckenberg, *op.cit.*, 114.
148   *Ibid.*, 129 and R.H. Kiernan, *op.cit.*, 172. In a speech Smuts gave to the British Houses of Parliament in 1943, he described Hitler as follows: "He has started a new era of martyrdom for the human spirit, an era of persecution such as mankind has not known since its emergence from the Dark Age. The suffering he has inflicted on Jews and Christians alike, the tide of horrors launched under his Gestapo régime over the fair West, constitute the darkest page of modern history. He has outraged and insulted and challenged the very spirit of humanity and tried to found a new barbarism". The real horrors and the grotesque crimes and atrocities, which the Judeo-Bolsheviks had been inflicting on the Russian people in the Soviet Union for over 20 years, appeared to have escaped Smuts' attention.
149   His home language was German.
150   On his second visit to Germany Pirow drove through the centre of Berlin with Hitler. The streets were lined with over a million well wishers. A part of his mission had been to ease the tension on the Jewish issue in Germany. On 14 January 1952 Associated Press reported that Pirow had said in a speech in Johannesburg that "Chamberlain had told him that he was under great pressure from World Jewry not to accommodate Hitler."
151   S.M. Goodson, *A Goodson Illustrated Guide Adolf Hitler & The Third Reich*, The Barnes Review, Washington D.C., 2009, 23-5 and www.veteranstoday.com/2011/09/13/hitler-and-the-banksters-the-abolition-of-interest-servitude

Smuts was equally ignorant of European affairs. He described the *Anschluss* between Austria and Germany as "a display of brute force which amounted simply to the rape of Austria".[152] Yet not a single life was lost and in a plebiscite held on 10 April 1938, 99.7% of the voters in Austria agreed to unification with Germany and rule by the party of Adolf Hitler.

Adolf Hitler announcing the *Anschluss* to the people of Austria at the Heldenplatz in Vienna, 15 March 1938. He was greeted with great enthusiasm and jubilation in contrast to Smuts' allegation that Germany had used "brute force" and had "raped" Austria.

On 24 March 1933 World Jewry made a world-wide declaration of war on Germany.[153] Understandably, Jews were no longer welcome to stay in Germany and started to emigrate. As previously noted, already since the days of the *Het Volk* government in 1907, Smuts had been encouraging Jewish immigration into South Africa. According to H.C. Armstrong "Smuts had a personal liking for Jews; he liked them round

---

152   P.B. Blanckenberg, *op.cit.*, 124.
153   The headlines of the *Daily Express*, Friday, 24 March 1933, read as follows: "Judea Declares War on Germany Jews Of All The World Unite In Action." *The New York Times* had similar headlines.

him......But above all Smuts shared with the Jews their tremendous arrogance."[154] In a speech given at a Zionist banquet in Johannesburg in May 1938, Smuts spoke about "his special love for Jewry" [155] and described the rebuilding of a Jewish National Home in Palestine as "the most romantic cause in the world to-day.[156]

In 1937 Prime Minister JBM Hertzog (1866-1942) introduced a bill to curtail Jewish immigration to South Africa and to regulate the right of any person to assume a surname. Amendments proposed by Dr. Daniel Francois Malan (1874-1959), leader of the *Gesuiwerde Nasionale Party* (Purified National Party), to specifically prohibit Jewish immigration, to end further naturalization of Jewish permanent residents and to exclude certain professions from Jews were unsuccessful. Nonetheless, in spite of Smuts' opposition, the Aliens Act was passed in February 1937. In 1940 Dr. Malan accused Smuts of turning South Africa into a "Jewish-imperialistic war machine" and in speeches made during World War II, he often referred to Smuts as "Smutskowitz" [157].

During 1938 General Hertzog sent a number of cables to Adolf Hitler apologising for the lies and distortions which were being published in the largely Jewish-controlled English language press.[158] At the time of the Czechoslovakian crisis in September 1938, Smuts and Hertzog had agreed that South Africa would remain neutral in the event of hostilities commencing in Europe.

On 1 September 1939 Germany was forced into interceding on behalf of the one and half million Germans living in Poland, after thousands of Germans had been mercilessly slaughtered by the Poles in clear acts of provocation.

---

154   H.C. Armstrong, *op.cit.*, 300.
155   P.B. Blanckenberg, *op.cit.*, 173.
156   *Ibid.*, 173.
157   R. Kraus, *op.cit.*, 368. "Smutskowitz" was first coined by Eric Holm on Radio Zeesen, Germany.
158   J.C. Smuts (Jnr.), *op.cit.*, 371.

Oswald Pirow, minister of defence, visited Adolf Hitler twice in 1933 and 1938. Seen here walking past a Luftwaffe guard of honour with to his left, Admiral Wilhelm Canaris, and to his right, Lieutenant-General Ernst Seifert, Kommandant of Berlin, November 1938.

On the evening of 2 September 1939 an emergency cabinet meeting was convened at the prime minister's residence, Groote Schuur. For nearly three hours Hertzog argued, without notes, in favour of neutrality. He ridiculed the notion that Hitler was out for world domination and insisted that he wished to reverse the injustices of the Treaty of Versailles. He contended that the Polish question was a purely local problem in Eastern Europe. He said that Britain could continue to use the naval base of Simon's Town, but that South Africa should remain neutral. Smuts, the pawn of the international bankers, challenged this logical argument with the absurd claim that German action in Poland was in reality a threat to the security of the whole world.

World War II Recruitment poster

On 5 September 1939 the drama unfolded in parliament. Hertzog had five cabinet ministers who supported him, while Smuts had six. The vote count was 80 in favor of war, 67 against. Just seven votes would have swung the result the other way.

Hertzog a genuine patriot, whose principle since 1912 had always been "South Africa First", tried to impose martial law and to prorogue parliament until 3 February 1940. He demanded that the Governor-General, Sir Patrick Duncan (a former member of Lord Milner's *Kindergarten*)[159] and a "complacent admirer" [160] (of Smuts) announce an immediate general election with the obvious intention of declaring South Africa's neutrality while parliament was in recess. However, this request was refused and Hertzog resigned.

159   A group of mainly upper class Englishmen brought to South Africa in 1902 by Lord Milner to set up a South African Civil Service.
160   Armstrong, *op.cit.*, 359.

South Africa had no vital interests or concerns in the events taking place in Eastern Europe. When Hitler heard of South Africa's declaration of war, he reportedly burst out laughing;[161] and not surprisingly so. The entire South African defence force had 5,385 permanent force members and two demonstration models of World War I tanks, while the air force consisted of two Blenheim bombers and 26 obsolete Hawker Furies and Harts.[162] The South African Naval Service had three officers and three ratings and an engineless training ship, the *General Botha*. 12,000 South Africans would eventually die in this senseless, fratricidal conflict, including an uncle of the author who was killed by shrapnel in Rome on 6 June 1944.

Large numbers of Afrikaners and English-speaking South Africans were against Smuts' servile declaration of war,[163] which was in the sole interest of the international bankers, who wished to destroy Germany's usury-free banking system, and later those of Italy and Japan too.[164]

In June 1939 Dr. Arthur Pillans Laurie, professor of chemistry and a Fellow of the Royal Society of Edinburgh, highlighted in *The Case for Germany. A Study of Modern Germany* the principal reason why England was compelled to start a war with Germany.

> "As long as Germany and Italy are under their present governments, they will not touch foreign loans, and Germany by her method of internal economy and trading has eliminated the international financier, and those who make profits by playing with foreign exchanges. That is doubtless why the government is being forced by the 'City' to start a trade war with Germany.

---

161 J.C. Smuts (Jnr.), *op.cit.*, 381.
162 *Ibid.*, 381.
163 Smuts' unpopularity extended to troops in the field. According to S.E.D. Brown, who served as an intelligence officer in Cairo censoring mail, on one occasion when a number of skits on World War II leaders had been made at an entertainment show for South African troops, the one on Smuts was booed by the whole audience. It may also be noted that more than half the servicemen who served in North Africa were not prepared to take the General Service Oath to serve anywhere in the world. J. Bourhill and F. Pretorius, How the story of the South African experience in the Italian campaign was recorded – and distorted, *Historia*, 57.2., November 2012, 366. See also E. Axelson, *A Year in Italy: An Account of a Year as Military Historian with the South African 6th Armoured Division in Italy, 1944-1945*, Self-published, 2004, 254 pp.
164 S.M. Goodson, The Real Reason the Japanese Attacked Pearl Harbor, *The Barnes Review*, Washington D.C., Vol. XIV No.6, November/December 2008, 41-5 and www.veteranstoday.com/2011/06/26was-world-war-ii-fought-to-make-the-world-safe-for-usury

If the economic methods devised by Germany are successful, and spread to other nations, and if Hitler succeeds in his policy of establishing permanent peace in Europe, the high financier will cease to be able to exist. It is therefore their main interest today to plunge the four powers into war, in order to destroy Germany and Italy".[165]

Foremost amongst those organisations against Smuts were the *Gryshemde* (Grey Shirts) also known as the South African Gentile National Socialist Movement, which had been founded by Louis Weichardt in 1933. Another prominent organisation was the *Ossewa-Brandwag* (Ox wagon Sentinel), which at its peak had 275,000 members[166] and was led by Dr. Johannes Frederik Janse van Rensburg, a former administrator of the Orange Free State and secretary of justice under Smuts. Van Rensburg, who was a fluent speaker of German, became an admirer of national socialism after having visited Germany and having met Adolf Hitler and Hermann Göring. Numerous acts of sabotage, such as the blowing up of railway lines and power and telephone lines were perpetrated. Some of the leaders of the *Ossewa-Brandwag* were imprisoned at Koffiefontein, a diamond mining town in the south west of the Orange Free State, and one of the more notable detainees was Balthazar Johannes Vorster, who would later become prime minister (1966-1978). The *Ossewa-Brandwag* had been founded as a cultural organization in 1938 at the time of the 150th anniversary of the Great Trek. During World War II it adopted political ambitions. According to Advocate P.J. Pretorius a senior member of National Intelligence, unknown to most of its well intentioned followers, it was a front, which had been created by Smuts and Colonel J.C.C. Laas, a freemason, in order to provide an escape valve and to split the conservative Afrikaners.[167]

165   http://www.wintersonnenwende.com/scriptorium/english/archives/caseforgermany/cfg00.html
166   P.J. Pretorius, *op.cit.*, 103.
167   *Ibid*, 309. On 7 July 1973, the National Party government set up the *Afrikaner Weerstandsbeweging* (Afrikaner Resistance Movement) in order to channel and contain right wing concerns and resentment in a similar manner to the establishment of the *Ossewa-Brandwag*. Other fronts established by the government at this time included the Conservative Party (1982) and the Freedom Front (1994). The car of the leader of the latter organization, Constand Viljoen, was frequently seen parked outside the residence of President F.W. de Klerk; just as the vehicle of Hans van Rensburg of the OB was often seen parked at the house of Smuts.

Vorster would use his two years in detention in order to burnish his right wing and nationalist credentials, like Smuts did during the Anglo-Boer War. He was in fact a clandestine liberal, who had been brainwashed by Professor Mortie Malherbe, a freemason, while he was studying law at the University of Stellenbosch (1934-38). Vorster was a paid Smuts agent,[168] who had been instructed to penetrate the *Ossewa-Brandwag* under false pretences. Prior to his internment at Koffiefontein he was imprisoned at Pretoria Central jail, where he had received weekly visits from Julius First, the father-in-law of the later secretary general of the South African Communist Party, Joe Slovo (real name Yossel Mashel Slovotnik).[169] Again, according to P.J. Pretorius on 26 July 1961 Vorster was recruited as an intelligence agent of the CIA.[170] Later he would be deeply implicated in the murder of Prime Minister Dr. Hendrik Frensch Verwoerd (1958-1966).[171]

Winston Churchill and Jannie Smuts. Smuts was one of the few men to whom Churchill would defer and seek advice.

As early as 1940, it had been proposed that in the event of Churchill's death or incapacitation, Smuts would be appointed British prime minister. Both King George VI and Queen

---

168   P.J. Pretorius, *op. cit.*, 143. In February 1938 after he had received his training, Vorster was paid £1,000 prior to his penetration of the *Ossewa-Brandwag*. On pages 72-73 there is an affidavit written by J.A.W. (Jan) Esterhuyzen (Junior) whose father was interned with Vorster in the same bungalow (No. 10) at Koffiefontein in 1942. In his affidavit Esterhuyzen attests that Vorster received monthly visits from Julius First. He also states that when the prisoners dug a tunnel in order to escape and had reached the perimeter, Vorster tipped off the commandant about the intended breakout.

169   F. Richter, *Vlug Vir Die Strafgerig*, Libanon-Uitgewers, Mosselbaai, Western Cape, 1995, 122.

170   *Ibid.*, 145.

171   *Ibid.*, 156-65 and J.A. Marais, *Die Era van Verwoerd*, Aktuele Publikasies, Pretoria, 1992, 185-99.

Elizabeth were in agreement with this proposal. [172]

On 22 June 1940 after the capitulation of France, General Hertzog proposed that peace be made with Germany and Italy and that South Africa accept Germany's peace initiatives. Smuts rejected this peace offer and in his usual high-handed manner, did so without consulting parliament. [173] Although South Africa ended its state of war with Germany on 9 July 1951, a peace treaty has still not been signed.

On 25 June 1940 Churchill sent a cipher telegram Circular D. No. 340 MOST SECRET to the prime ministers of Australia, Canada, New Zealand and South Africa as to whether peace should be negotiated with Germany. The British war cabinet was deeply divided about concluding a peace treaty. In his reply Smuts, who was venerated by Churchill, urged the latter not to entertain any discussions about peace, as they would result in a usury-free "Schacht currency system" and be a "political disaster of the first water". (See Appendix pages 74-75). This raises the intriguing supposition that Smuts bears responsibility for having prolonged the European War and the unnecessary deaths of over 50 million people. If Smuts had supported Germany's peace proposals, which principally entailed withdrawal of all German forces from Western Europe, with the exception of those areas having a German majority, and allowing Germany a free hand in the East, there appears to be little doubt that Churchill would have followed his advice. The quotations in the appendix clearly indicate the irresistible influence which Smuts held over Churchill.

Smuts, who was appointed a Field Marshal by the British government on 30 April 1941 did not play a direct role in World War II military operations, but on his four extended visits to England during the war, he was always invited to attend cabinet meetings. He made numerous speeches, rallying the British people to continue fighting until "victory" had been achieved in this fratricidal war.

In October 1941 Smuts "donated" 54 tons of South Africa's gold reserves valued at £20 million (£128 billion in to-day's values) at Churchill's request in order to shore up Britain's crumbling finances. As in the past, Smuts once again consulted neither his cabinet colleagues nor parliament. One month later the USS Quincy, a cruiser with a top speed of 33 knots, collected the gold at Simon's Town and shipped it via Trinidad

172   J. Colville, *The Fringes of Power: Downing Street Diaries*, Hodder & Stoughton, London, 1985, 269-71. In the event of Smuts being appointed prime minister, he would have been elevated to the House of Lords.
173   R.H. Kiernan, *op.cit.*, 152.

The cruiser, *USS Quincy* (12,463 tons), was used to ship 54 tons of South African gold from Simon's Town to New York. On 9 August 1942 she was sunk off Savo Island by the Japanese navy with heavy loss of life.

to New York, where it was deposited into Rothschild's privately-owned US Federal Reserve Bank.[174]

Smuts' assessment of the other allied wartime leaders displayed naiveté. Even while the Soviet army was rampaging through Eastern Europe with fatal consequences for all of its inhabitants, he was moved to say that he "doffs his cap to Stalin".[175] His opinion of Franklin D. Roosevelt was expressed in similar vein. In a letter to a friend in March 1937, he wrote that "Roosevelt is a remarkable man",[176] while his son J.C. Smuts writes in his father's biography: "The impression he formed then, and the one he carried through life, was that Roosevelt was a man of great courage. He admired his long, dogged struggle against adverse public opinion and isolationism, and the way he finally brought America into the war, albeit with the providential help of Pearl Harbor".[177]

In December 1943 Smuts was severely criticised by the French press after he claimed that France had lost her position as a Great Power.

As the war drew to its catastrophic conclusion, Germany was being obliterated from the skies by the barbarous "Butcher" Harris, chief of the Royal Air Force's Bomber Command.

---

174 P.J. Buchanan, *Churchill, Hitler and "the unnecessary war": how Britain lost its empire and the West lost the world*, Random House, 2008, 408. During 1941 there was a temporary peak in gold production of 450 tons and thus the request for 54 tons was easily accommodated out of current production. See C.J.H. Hartnady, South Africa's gold production and reserves, *South African Journal of Science*, 105, September/October 2009, 328.
175 En.wikipedia.org/wiki/South_African_general_election,_1948
176 P.B. Blanckenberg, *op.cit.*, 75.
177 J.C. Smuts (Jnr.), *op.cit.*, 469.

This bombing insanity would culminate on February 13/14 in the holocaust of Dresden, an undefended city packed with refugees, in which at least 300 000 victims perished, 75% of them women and children.[178] In 1915 Harris, a bugler in the 1st Battalion Rhodesia Regiment, had fought with Smuts in the South West Africa campaign.[179]

Smuts, who wrote the preamble to the United Nations, signing the charter in San Francisco on 26 June 1945.

Smuts increasingly devoted his energies to the establishment of the United Nations Organization (UN), which would provide the framework for the new world order. At the Dumbarton Oaks, Washington D.C. conference held from 21 August – 7 October 1944 to set up the UN, Smuts played a significant role in persuading Churchill and Roosevelt to accept Stalin's insistence on the right of a Great Power to veto decisions of the Security Council.[180] He was an active participant at the conference held in San Francisco in April 1945 and was responsible for drafting the preamble to the United Nations Charter. On 19 May 1945 he unveiled a memorial plaque in honour of Franklin D. Roosevelt at Muir Woods Cathedral Grove outside San Francisco.

---

178 D. Irving, *The Destruction of Dresden*, Futura Publications Limited, London, 1980, 259-60. According to the Order of the Day No. 47 signed at Dresden on 22 March 1945, by Colonel Grosse, up to the evening of 20 March 1945, 202,040 bodies had been recovered, of which only 30% could be identified. It was further assumed that the death roll would climb to at least 250,000.

179 Sir Arthur Travers Harris was a Rhodesian tobacco farmer who always considered himself to be a Rhodesian. After World War II Harris tried to become governor of Southern Rhodesia, but was turned down as there was no vacancy available at that time. Instead he settled in South Africa and worked as managing director of South African Marine Corporation (1946-1953). Afterwards he bought a residence in the seaside village of St James, near Cape Town, and spent the English winters there.

180 P. Beukes, *op.cit.*, 180.

However, as early as 31 March 1947 in a letter to an American friend, Mr. F. Lamont, Smuts expressed his grave disappointment in the United Nations "not only personally, but from the larger viewpoint which we have at heart".[181] His disenchantment was undoubtedly reinforced by the UN's refusal two months earlier to permit the incorporation of South West Africa into South Africa; notwithstanding the fact that in a referendum held between May and June 1946, 85.5% of the territory's indigenous inhabitants had voted for such a measure.

Harry Oppenheimer (1908-2000), a confederate of the Rothschilds, who recorded in the April-June 1960 issue of *Africa South* that Smuts had "served us well".

In February - April 1947 Smuts hosted the British Royal family on an official tour of South Africa and its neighbouring territories. Smuts hoped that this visit would increase his prestige and boost his party's chances of winning the following year's general election. Instead it introduced a divisive element into white politics. The leader of the opposition, Dr. D.F. Malan (later prime minister 1948-54), refused to meet King George, while *Die Transvaler* newspaper, under the editorship of Dr. H.F. Verwoerd, did not report on the visit.

---

181   *Ibid.*, 131.

The final word in this chapter is reserved for Harry Oppenheimer, the scion of super capitalism in South Africa during the latter half of the twentieth century. In 1960 in an article titled Portrait of a Millionaire: I, Harry Oppenheimer in the magazine *Africa South* written in the first person, Oppenheimer wrote: "Smuts **served us well**…, but since 1948, I must admit, we have been floundering. The United Party was quite hopeless."[182]

---

182 H. F. Oppenheimer, A Portrait of a Millionaire: I, Harry Oppenheimer, *Africa South*, April-June 1960, Vol. 4, no. 3, 14.

Chapter IX

SMUTS' ZIONISM

One of Smuts' last acts before he lost power in the 26 May 1948 election, was to ensure that South Africa was one of the first countries to recognize Israel as a *de facto* state on 24 May 1948. He had been an ardent Zionist since he helped draft the Balfour Declaration. This provides an opportune moment to reflect on Smuts' close relationship with Jews, and Zionists in particular.

In 1914 Smuts was appointed legal adviser to the South African Jewish Board of Deputies. He first met Chaim Weizmann, the second prime minister of Israel, when the latter was professor of chemistry at the University of Manchester in 1917. Their friendship would flourish until Smuts' death.

In early 1918 Smuts travelled via Rome to Palestine, where he met the commander of the Egyptian Expeditionary Force, General Edmund Allenby, in order to consult with him about his final advance, which revolved around Haifa and Damascus.

At the Versailles Peace Conference Smuts acted as a secret agent for Weizmann, reporting "on all that went on in the chambers of power".[183] He also drafted the regulations for the Class A mandate for Palestine. The final version was edited by Felix Frankfurter, an Associate Justice of the Supreme Court of the United States (1939-62).

---

183 W. Tansill, A Study in Zionist-Gentile Cooperation, a book review of *Weizmann and Smuts: A Study in Zionist-South African Co-operation* by Richard P. Stevens, *Cultural Review*, PVP, California, Sept/Oct 2002, 47-51. This friendship between Smuts and Weizmann is also confirmed by a former chairman of the South African Zionist Federation, Nicolai Kirschner, in Zionism and the Union of South Africa: Fifty Years of Friendship and Understanding, *Jewish Affairs*, South Africa, May 1960, where he states that "There is a particular dimension to this secret consort between Balfour and the Zionist leadership to betray the aspirations of the Palestinian people. It was Weizmann's close friend and future prime minister of South Africa, General Jan Smuts, who, as a South African delegate to the British Cabinet during World War I, helped push the British government to adopt the Balfour Declaration and to make a commitment to construct a Zionist colony under British direction."

At the San Remo Conference in January 1920 Smuts telegraphed to Lloyd George, whose legal firm, Lloyd George, Roberts and Co., represented the Zionists' interests in England, Jewish demands for the mandated territory to include the Litani and Jordan rivers, increased immigration and industrial and agricultural developments. In 1928 Smuts was offered the post of High Commissioner of Palestine, but after due consideration declined, as he felt that his highest duty lay in South Africa. The position was taken by Sir John Chancellor, a former governor of Southern Rhodesia (1923-1928).

In October 1930 the Colonial Secretary, Lord Passfield (Sidney Webb), wrote a White Paper after the 1929 Arab riots, recommending an end to discriminatory labour practices by the Zionists and a more pro-Arab position. These proposals threw the Zionists into a "frenzy"[184] and once again Smuts was roped in by Weizmann. At a meeting with Passfield, Smuts warned him that "historic justice" [185] towards the Jews required him to protect them and that he should not "go on drifting".[186] These sentiments were repeated in a letter to *The Times* signed by Smuts, Lord Balfour and Lloyd George. Ramsay MacDonald the British prime minister soon caved in.

There were further widespread Arab riots in 1937. The Peel Commission was appointed to investigate and "found great merit in the Arab complaints about Zionism"[187] and recommended that immigration be suspended. The Commission also proposed that the territory be partitioned, with 80% of the land being allocated to the Arabs and 20% to the Jews. Smuts was again enlisted and wrote strongly worded letters to Lord Harlech (William Ormsby-Gore), the Colonial Secretary, demanding that he reverse the intended policy.

Simultaneously on 9 November 1938 Zionists from France staged a 'false flag' operation in Germany later known as *Kristallnacht* (Night of Broken Glass) in order to gain world-wide sympathy for Jews and to scare them into fleeing Germany – preferably to Palestine. The British parliament was about to adopt legislation guaranteeing Palestine to the Palestinians. A German diplomat

---

184   *Ibid.*, 48.
185   *Ibid.*, 48.
186   *Ibid.*, 48.
187   *Ibid.*, 49.

in Paris by a deranged Polish Jew at the behest of a Jewish organization known as the *International League Against Anti-Semitism* (LICA), which was established in 1927, originally as The League Against Pogroms.

False telephone and telegram instructions were issued by *agents provocateurs* to *Kreisleiters* (district leaders) and other junior leaders to set alight Jewish businesses and synagogues. Unfortunately some of them did respond, and a large number of buildings were burnt down, and 89 people are alleged to have died. Hitler was infuriated when he heard about this outrage and ordered that it be stopped immediately. [188]

When a White Paper of 1939 proposed a cessation of all immigration "Smuts, ever faithful, once again rushed to the rescue". Throughout World War II Smuts was Weizmann's "obedient Zionist watchdog".[189]

During the fighting in Palestine (1946-1948) large numbers of Jewish South African pilots participated in the war against the British and the indigenous Arab inhabitants. According to Gary Giveser, whose father served as a pilot in the Israeli Air Force, Smuts was its founding father.[190]

In recognition of his magnificent services to the State of Israel, several streets have been named after Smuts, as well as the *kibbutz* Ramat Yohanan, which was founded in 1932 in the Valley of Zebulun, in the shadow of Mount Carmel. When Smuts was presented with the certificate recording the naming of the settlement after him, he declared: "This document will go down in my family as one of my most sacred possessions…. When I am disheartened (and I am never really disheartened), when South Africa does not seem to rise to the occasion, I shall go to that valley in Palestine which bears my name for inspiration". [191]

In 1949 a bust of Smuts by Moses Kottler was presented to the Hebrew University of Jerusalem. During that same year Smuts attended a service in Israel to commemorate his lifelong services to Zionism where he said: "The Middle East has been asleep for

188   I. Weckert, *Feuerzeichen: der "Reichskristallnacht", Anstifter und Brandstifter – Opfer und Nutzniesser*, Grabert Verlag, Tübingen, 1981, 301 pp.
189   W. Tansill, *op.cit.*, 50.
190   http://www.2facetruth.com/smuts-father-of-israel-air-force-re-gary-giveser-on-it-is-all-about-appearances-re-they-just-dont-give-a-damn-2/ Smuts was thus the founding father of three air forces: the Israeli Air Force, the Royal Air Force and the South African Air Force.
191   M. Gitlin, *The Vision Amazing The Story of South African Zionism*, The Menorah Book Club, Johannesburg, 1950, 199.

Bust of Jan Smuts which was installed in the Hebrew University of Jerusalem in 1949.

centuries, and I want to see Israel emerge as the vital force, leading its neighbouring countries along the paths of progress. It is this I want to see and not strife and warfare. It is my wish that we will soon witness the dawn of a new era in the Middle East, with Israel exerting a tremendous good." [192] During his lifetime Smuts supported his *idée fixe* by personally fundraising for multiple Zionist organisations.[193]

Wayne Tansill writes: "In this final testament of sublime falsity, Jan Christian Smuts established a standard of moral turpitude which has been followed faithfully by legions of western democratic politicians ever since. That was the measure of his achievement and the measure of the pure evil he served in the name of good".[194]

For all his great intellect, Smuts never realized that the Jews he slavishly served had no entitlement to claim the land of Palestine on historic grounds. Over 90% of the Jews living in Israel are Ashkenazim, who are descended from a non-Semitic people originally from present day southern Russia. In the eighth century A.D. King Bulan,

192   W. Tansill, *op.cit.*, 51.
193   J. Hunter, *Israeli Foreign Policy: South Africa and Central America*, South End Press, Boston, Massachusetts, 1987, 21-22.
194   W. Tansill, *op.cit.*, 51.

Harvest celebration at the kibbutz Ramat Yohanan in north western Israel, which was named after leading Zionist supporter, Jan Smuts.

converted his unruly pagan Turkic-Mongoloid people of Khazaria to Judaism, after having rejected Christianity and Mohammedanism as alternatives. [195]

195 *Jewish Jewish Encyclopaedia*, Funk and Wagnalls, New York, 1906, 7. Further confirmation may be found in an article on craniometry by Dr. Maurice Fishberg in the *Jewish Encyclopaedia IV*, 1902, 31-5. This study of nearly 3,000 Jewish heads from a wide variety of countries over a 20 year period, revealed that they were all brachycephalic or broad-headed with a cephalic index above 80; in contrast to the heads of the Arabs, which are dolicephalic or long-headed. See also Arthur Koestler, *The Thirteenth Tribe*, Popular Library, New York, 1976, 255 pp. and Shlomo Sand, *The Invention of the Jewish People*, Verso, New York, 2009, 344 pp. and *The Invention of the Land of Israel: From Holy Land to Homeland*, Verso, New York, 2012, 304 pp. The etymological origin of Khazaria is Qasar which is from the Turkish root qaz meaning to roam.

Chapter X

CONCLUSION

Smuts died of a coronary thrombosis at his home in Irene outside Pretoria on 11 September 1950. We may now pause to consider what Smuts' accomplishments were and whether he bestowed any benefits on South Africa. There is little doubt that he had a distinguished career as an international statesman, and was showered with many honours, including 29 honorary doctorates.

Statue of General Smuts in Parliament Square, London which was sculpted by Sir Jacob Epstein. The pedestal was made of South African granite.

However, Smuts' conduct in South Africa can only be described as harmful and at times even treasonous. He inveigled South Africa into three major wars. He treated South Africa's workers with contempt and was responsible for the killing of 535 white and 152 black miners. He introduced the unnecessary income tax and allowed a central bank to be set up, which enabled private banks to exploit the people ruthlessly through usury, which ultimately led to the white population capitulating in April 1994 to the detriment of everyone. He encouraged the settling of the worst type of Jewish immigrant from Lithuania, whose communist members would later play a leading role in destroying South Africa and handing the country over to the international bankers.[196] He failed to achieve reconciliation between Afrikaners[197] and English-speaking South Africans. Smuts was not only unpopular amongst a large section of the white population, but amongst black people too.[198] He lacked vision, unlike for example, Colonel Charles Frampton Stallard, leader of the Dominion Party, who drew up a master plan for the resolution of the racial question.[199] Colonel Stallard (1871-1971), who in many ways foreshadowed Dr. Hendrik Verwoerd, believed that the only way to do justice to blacks and whites was for each population group to inhabit its own territory, as blacks were completely unsuited to an urban existence and needed their tribal system and family structures to be strengthened, while those blacks who wished to work in the mines and on the farms on a temporary basis could continue to do so. Coloureds and Asians would eventually form part of the white group.

This tragic man consistently neglected to put South Africa first, but was instead fanatically devoted his entire life to the British Empire and the New World Order and worked tirelessly in the interests of his masters – the British/Zionist/Rothschild nexus. After his defeat in the general election held on 26 May 1948,

---

196 After the nominal takeover of South Africa by the African National Congress in April 1994, the South African Navy changed all the names of its six strike craft, named after previous ministers of defence, except the *SAS Jan Smuts*. In Cape Town, Durban, East London and Johannesburg streets and highways named in honour of Smuts have not been renamed.

197 The Transvalers dislike for Smuts was reflected in a popular song at that time where he was described as the *pienk piccanin* (the British little black boy).

198 "It will surprise many people outside South Africa to hear that General Smuts, great statesman though he was, was not particularly well liked by the Bantu, while Dr. Malan and Dr. Verwoerd, and the other leaders of their government have had the Bantus' respect. This is because General Smuts was never straight with us – he never had a clear-cut policy which we could understand, he never gave us anything to hope and live for – while the present government, for all its faults, is at least doing something definite to help us." C. Mutwa, *My People: Writings of a Zulu Witchdoctor*, Penguin Books Ltd, Johannesburg, 1971, 329.

199 H.R. Abercrombie, *Africa's Peril The Colour Problem*, Simpkin Marshall Ltd, London, 1938, 178-184. Hugh Romilly Abercrombie (1872-1955), a former president of the Transvaal Agricultural Union and the Pretoria Chamber of Commerce, proposed similar policies in an appendix titled *Programme of Principles of the Council of Europeans of Africa*.

Smuts finally realised that his work had all been in vain when he uttered this painful lament: "My work seems to go on and on and lead to nowhere".[200]

The life and career of J.C. Smuts can serve as a parable of the way Western thinking and political decisions have been corrupted up to the present day. The physical and psychic harm caused to the Western world by top personalities working against the interests of their own people - whether they realised it or not - is incalculable.

Many years ago when I commenced studying at the University of Stellenbosch, I was puzzled by the fact that previous prime ministers, who had studied there like Malan and Verwoerd had buildings named after them, but not Smuts. Now I know why.

---

200   T.E.W. Schumann, The *Abdication of the White Man*, Tafelberg Uitgewers, 1963, 149.

Map of South Africa 1899

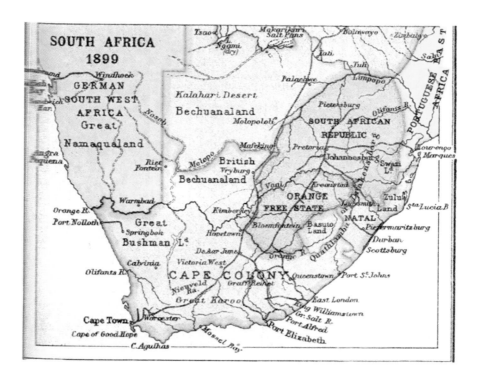

AFFIDAVIT

I Jan Adriaan Wilhemus Esterhuyzen ID No. 2702135021086 do hereby document a sworn affidavit on this the 27th day of November 2012 concerning the grandfather of my two sons Johann and Petrus Esterhuyzen in order to honour his memory.

On a cold winter afternoon in 1941 I returned home from Pietersburg High School only to be informed by our Bantu washerwoman that shortly after I departed for school that morning the South African Police arrived.

They searched through our entire house before taking both my parents away with them in a police van. I spent the entire afternoon painfully speculating on what my parents could have done to deserve being arrested. Meanwhile I waited in anguish for someone to turn up and set my tortured mind at ease.

After what seemed like an eternity the police arrived at dusk with my mother carrying a huge brown-paper parcel in her arms. She informed me that we were to say farewell to my father Jan Adriaan Johannes Esterhuyzen at 21h00 on the platform of Pietersburg railway station as he was to be escorted to Koffiefontein Internment Camp in the Free State. Mother had caringly obtained warm underclothing for my Dad who was unaccustomed to bitterly cold Free State winters!

At 21h00 two members of the Truth Legion escorted my father to a railway compartment. I was allowed to bid him farewell as he leant through the window of their compartment. He then appointed me as the 'man of the house' whose responsibility it was to take good care of my mother! I was only sixteen!

My father was an employee of the South African Railways and Harbours as a Leading Hand Communicatiions Technician who`s responsiblity it was to ensure that all telephone, telegraph and signal lines were fully operational so running times of trains could be scheduled and avoid accidents.

When communication lines between railway stations were sabotaged the suspicion immediately fell upon my father due to his intimate knowledge of the system. However sabotage continued after his internment so that he was released after two years at the end of 1943, due to intervention on his behalf by advocate Jerling. I owe it to my dear mother who found employment to provide for our needs. I also owe it to her that I matriculated in 1945.

Yes! My father was released but he was not reinstated in his former position with the SAR&H. He was a very proud man and a 'glutton for hard work' as his brother-in-law Adolf Couzyn described him. He was soon employed by a wealthy medical doctor A.J.K Holmes as his farm manager on Novengilla close to Letaba station.

When Smuts was defeated in 1948 and the Nationalists took over the reins of our country, my father was reinstated in his former position with the SAR&H. He was stationed at Letaba and was responsible for the maintenance of communication lines and cables between Duivelskloof and Komatiepoort on the border of Mocambique. He held this position until 1957 when he retired on pension to St. Michael's on Sea near Port Shepstone.

There are events which I must emphasize. Prior to the outbreak of World War II in September 1939 my father was recruited as a member of the Ossewa Brandwag by one Hendrik Alberts, a colleague on the SAR&H. However my father got wind of Alberts' association with Freemasonry and immediately resigned from the OB! After his release from Koffiefontein my father often cited Hans van Rensburg the leader of the Ossewa Brandwag as being hand-in-glove with Gen.Smuts. He supplied Smuts with the names of ardent members of this 'sham' organization which were eventually interned!

In Koffiefontein my father was housed with seven other internees in the same bungalow. They included dr.Trümpelman, dr. B.M. Kranz who painted the portrait of my father, and the renegade B.J Vorster who undoubtedly was to blame for the appointment of Dimitri Tsafendas, dr Verwoerd's assasin, in Parlaiment in September 1966!

On several occasions my father related to my mother and I how Balthazar John Vorster was regularly summoned to the Camp Commandant's office in Koffiefontein under the pretence of discussing business with his partner in a legal firm in Brakpan, Julius Fürst. But shortly after such a visit the internees were assembled on the parade ground, covered by machine guns in the towers. Soldiers then entered and upturned even the wooden floors of their bungalow's until a tunnel which they were digging in order to escape was discovered. My father spent two weeks in the 'cooler' for his participation in tunneling. This was a cell the size of an average W.C. with only a single bed matress and a lavatory bucket as furnishing. An elecric light bulb on the ceiling shone day and night. Only a Bible was allowed the prisoner! With only one blanket he almost froze to death in the Free State winter.

My Dad's incarceration cost our family dearly, and as result I was denied the privilege of attending a university. This treachery by fellow-Afrikaners has even had an effect on your lives even to this day!

I swear under oath that this is to the best of my knowledge a true record of your grandfather's experience of treachery in the ranks of fellow South Africans.

Date: 27/ 11/2012. Place: Citrusdal. W/Cape.

Signed: .... J.A. Esterhuyzen.

GEORGE HENDRIK MARAIS
Voortrekkerstraat | Voortrekker St 83
Citrusdal | Citrusdal
KOMMISSARIS VAN EDE
COMMISSIONER OF OATHS
PRAKTISERENDE PROKUREUR R.S.A.
PRACTISING ATTORNEY R.S.A.

Appendix

Cipher telegram from the Minister of External Affairs, Pretoria, to the High Commissioner, London. [General Smuts' reply] **Received - 6 p.m. 17th July 1940. No.547 Secret.**

"Circular D340 [message from Churchill] of June 25th raises a very important point which has troubled me for some time. It is most probable that Hitler will start a peace offensive at an early date. This may be either for a conference or some other form of peace propaganda.

...He will pose as the regenerator of an effete European system and will propose a United States of Europe composed of so called free states between whom tariff walls and economic barriers will have been abolished and only some such Schacht currency plan will exist.

...Some such scheme could be clothed in such plausible appearances as to make a formidable appeal to world public opinion already sickened of the horrible destruction of the war, and the spectre of the coming European famine. If, in addition, Hitler is big enough to renounce annexations and indemnities, its appeal may become irresistible and make Europe accept a peace which will be a moral and political disaster of the first water.

...Let brain trusts be set going to work out an alternate democratic plan for countering a peace movement which is certain to come sooner or later and, should find us prepared with the answer."

NB. Under the British Official Secrets Act, the files relating to the German peace proposals should have been released to the public in 2017, but in an unprecedented decision, they have been sealed for another 20 years.

Confirmation of Churchill's adulation for Smuts and his heavy reliance on the latter's advice, may be found in the following quotations extracted from W.S. Churchill, *The Second World War*, Cassell & Co. Ltd, London, 1948-1954.

"Please give your counsel, my old and valiant friend". Telegram from Churchill to Smuts, 9 June 1940, vol. ii, 130.

"I send you these personal notes in order to keep in closest contact with your thoughts, which ever weigh with me". Telegram from Churchill to Smuts, 27 June 1940, vol. ii, 193-194.

"It gives me so much pleasure and confidence to be trekking with you along the path we have followed for so many years". Telegram from Churchill to Smuts, 22 September 1940, vol. ii. 389.

"Most grateful for all your help, and above all for your surefooted judgement, which marches with our laboriously reached conclusions". Telegram from Churchill to Smuts, 12 January 1941, vol. iii, 31-32.

"Will you tell Smuts how glad I should be if now he is so near he could come and do a month's work in the War Cabinet as of old". Telegram from Churchill to Eden, 9 March 1941, vol. iii, 95.

"I wonder if you would care for me to suggest to the King your appointment as an Honorary Field-Marshal of the British Army. It seems to me that the great part you are playing in our military affairs and the importance of the South African Army would make this appropriate in every way, and I need not say how pleasing it would be to your old friend and comrade to pay you this compliment". Telegram from Churchill to Smuts, 8 May 1941, vol. iii, 594. (Churchill failed to mention the contribution of the South African Air Force, which at the decisive second battle of El Alamein in November 1942 provided half the air force).

"I am, as usual, in close sympathy and agreement with your military outlook". Telegram from Churchill to Smuts, 16 May 1941, vol. iii, 226-227.

"All the above is for your own most secret information". Telegram from Churchill to Smuts, 14 September 1941, vol. iii, 406.

"I had urged General Smuts to come from South Africa to the scene, and he was already at the Embassy [Cairo] when I arrived. We spent the morning together, and I told him all the troubles and the choices that were open", 4 August 1942, vol. iv, 374-375.

"General Smuts was with us at home in these days, and it was a comfort to find out how close was our agreement", 19 November 1942, vol. iv, 512.

"Smuts, who followed the Greek fortunes attentively, also sent a prescient comment", 20 August 1943, vol. v, 416-417.

"Field Marshal Smuts will be in Cairo Monday, September 27, staying with Casey [Minister of State Resident in Middle East], and will be in your theatre about four days later on his way here. He possesses my entire confidence, and everything can be discussed with him with the utmost freedom. He will stay some months in London, taking up his full duties as a member of the British War Cabinet. He will carry great weight here with public opinion. I shall be grateful if he is treated with the utmost consideration. He is a magnificent man and one of my most cherished friends". Telegram from Churchill to Eisenhower, 21 September 1943, vol. v, 126-127.

"Most earnestly do I look forward to seeing you and I rejoice that you will be at my side in momentous times". Telegram from Churchill to Smuts, 27 February 1944, vol. v, 383-384.

"On Monday, May 15 [1944], three weeks before D Day, we held a final conference in London at Montgomery's headquarters in St. Paul's School. The King, Field-Marshal Smuts, the British Chiefs of Staff, the commanders of the expedition, and many of their principal Staff officers were present", vol. v, 478.

"On the morning of Friday, June 2 [1944], I set out in my train for our siding by Eisenhower's headquarters near Portsmouth, with Field-Marshal Smuts, Mr. Ernest Bevin, General Ismay, and my personal staff", vol. v, 483.

"Smuts, who had now returned to South Africa, sent a prescient and suggestive telegram", 10 July 1944, vol. vi, 34.

"General Smuts' meditations at his farm in the veldt led him along the same paths of thought …", 20 September 1944, vol. vi, 181.

"I have read with great interest your telegram [of September 20] from Field-Marshal Smuts, and I think we are all in agreement with him as to the necessity of having the U.S.S.R. as a fully accepted and equal member of any association of the Great Powers formed for the purpose of preventing international war". Telegram from Roosevelt to Churchill, 28 September 1944, vol. vi, 185.

"I sent my comments on the whole situation to Smuts", 3 December 1944, vol. vi, 224-225.

"It was a pleasure to hear at the same time from one on whose judgement and instinct in such matters I relied", 14 December 1944, vol. vi, 251.

"I also received some wise advice from Smuts", 30 December 1944, vol. vi, 268.

Reviews

A very interesting work, indeed! We all know that Smuts was not a patriot. I can remember PW telling me [that] when he was a young politician and when walking down the corridors of Parliament, Smuts stopped him and said that he would become leader in this country. That was basically all PW had to do with Smuts. It amazes me how naïve the Boers were. However, can we blame them? They werenot as informed as we are today.

Barbara Botha, widow of PW Botha, President of the
Republic of South Africa (1978 to 1989)

IN the second year of my studies at London's Royal Academy of Music, the Wardencalled me to his office and introduced me to Lieutenant-General Sir (George) Sidney Clive GCVO, KCB, CMG, DSO (1874-1959), one of the Academy's Governors. I was asked to rehearse and then perform the Delius sonata for cello and piano to friends of a kind and generous patron of the Academy and was later to learn that his love of music, matched by an interest in the achievements of its students, was one reason why he wanted to meet me to discover what brought an Afrikaner to the Academy.

In the years that followed, our rehearsals often took place at 488 Finchley Road and although conversations between Sir Sidney and my mother usually ranged over a wide canvas, his comments concerning Jan Smuts may be of interest.

Unimpressed by the man's character but constrained by loyalty to his own country, as a military man Sir Sidney shared with others in the British army, like Lord Methuen, a distaste for Lord Kitchener's military tactics in the Anglo-Boer War.

On one occasion mother's sister (imprisoned with two other sisters and a brother in Bloemfontein's concentration camp), who had recently arrived from South Africa, asked Sir Sidney whether English people disliked Smuts as much as most Afrikaners did.

"I never knew what to make of Smuts," he replied. "However, I believe that his departure from the Cape was less to do with political intrigue in the Cape than adesire to acquire status and power. In the British Empire, it seemed to me that he had to appear to support the Afrikaner, especially after the Jameson Raid debacle of 1895, when he made it clear that in his opinion the actions of Milner, Phillips and Beit, as representatives of a British Connection, were harmful to South Africa's best interests."

But what exactly was Jan Smuts's role in the annihilation of the Afrikaner? For example, his secret memorandum dated September 4, 1899, states:

"South Africa stands on the eve of a frightful bloodbath out of which our people will emerge ... either as ... hewers of wood and drawers of water for a hated race, or as victors, founders of a united South Africa: of one of the great empires of the world ... an Afrikaner republic stretching from Table Bay to the Zambezi." How does this prophecy of gloom equate with his actions in support of Ernest Oppenheimer's decision in 1922 to limit the production of diamonds and gold in order to keep prices high? How could Smuts's use of machine guns to quell the anger of thousands of white workers who had been made redundant (and in which my father nearly lost his life) serve South Africa's best interests? Small wonder that Smuts's subservience to the country that had implemented Lord Milner's oft repeated plea that "The Afrikaner must be annihilated" earned the contempt of thousands of Afrikaners at the opening ceremony of the Voortrekker Monument in 1938. Stephen Goodson's booklet provides compelling evidence that bankers, financiers and entrepreneurs have been instrumental in destroying "Africa, the Last Continent With a Soul of its Own" (JJ Jung).

Alexander Kok, FRAM

A splendid piece of work.

Mario Pretorius, descendant of Andries Pretorius (1798-1853), founder of the Transvaal Republic

GOODSON is a former director of the South African Reserve Bank (2003-2012) and was for several months before the end of his tenure the target of considerable Jewish and other pressures due to his forthright articles describing the banking systems of Axis Germany and Japan.

Smuts is upheld in iconic terms among some interests, in the same manner as Churchill and Roosevelt, and for the same reasons. Goodson's book looks behind the myth and documents the career of Smuts as a traitor to his Boer folk, and everwilling to play his role in the service of Jews, Zionists and plutocracy. Lauded as a great statesman, Smuts was instrumental in the founding of the State of Israel, having been involved with the Balfour Declaration, the League of Nations and the United Nations Organisation, the preamble of the UN Charter having been written by him.

His theory of 'Holism' was formulated to provide a scientific or evolutionary basis for the doctrine of internationalism, based on the view that the joining of smaller parts to a greater whole leads to the strengthening of the new combination. The eventual outcome of such unions being a world state.

Smuts had been a leader of Boer forces but was remembered for his betrayal of the Boer cause, his avid commitment to the British Empire, and his unleashing of the South African military and air force on striking mineworkers on the Rand who were resisting the mine owners use of Black cheap labour. Their slogan was 'White workers of the world united for a White South Africa'. The conflict was a more overt manifestation of the inherent enmity that had existed between the Afrikaners and plutocracy, which finally resulted in the end of apartheid and the victory of Money [in 1994].

Smuts was under the same financial obligations as Winston Churchill to Sir Henry Strakosch, whom Smuts requested to draft the Act for the South African Reserve Bank, which set the Afrikaners on the road to usury bondage; while Churchill, whom Strakosch saved from bankruptcy, henceforth committed himself to war against Germany.

Smuts was one of the architects of the world political order as it has been shaped since World War I. Goodson's book explains the motivations.

Dr. Kerry Bolton, *Ab Aeterno,* Journal of the Academy of Social & Political Research, Greece, No. 14, Jan.-Mar. 2013, 37

YOUR book contains some perspectives which were quite unknown to me, so that there is much reason for gratitude.

Dr. Ernst Nolte, Professor emeritus of Modern History, Free University of Berlin

Bibliography

H.R. Abercrombie, *Africa's Peril The Colour Problem*, Simpkin Marshall Ltd, London, 1938.

H.R. Abercrombie, *The Secret History of South Africa or Sixty five years in the Transvaal*, Central News Agency Ltd, Johannesburg, 1952.

H.C. Armstrong, *Grey Steel J.C. Smuts A Study in Arrogance*, Arthur Barkers Ltd, London, 1937.

P. Beukes, *The Holistic Smuts A Study in Personality Foreward by H.F. Oppenheimer*, Human & Rousseau, Cape Town, 1989.

P.B. Blanckenberg, *The Thoughts of General Smuts*, Juta & Co. Limited, Cape Town, 1951.

L.J. Bothma, *Rebelspoor*, Self-published, Langenhovenpark, Orange Free State, 2015.

B.P. Bouwer, *Memoirs of General Bouwer*, Human Sciences Research Council, Pretoria, 1980.

P.J. Buchanan, *Churchill, Hitler and "the unnecessary war": how Britain lost its empire and the West lost the world*, Random House, 2008.

T. Cameron, *Jan Smuts, An illustrated biography*, Human & Rousseau, Cape Town, 1994.

W.S. Churchill, *The Second World War The Gathering Storm*, Vol. 1, Cassell & Co. Ltd, London, 1948.

F.S. Crafford, *Jan Smuts: A Biography*, Greenwood Publishing Group, Westport, Connecticut, 1968.

I. Colville, *The Fringes of Power: Downing Street Diaries 1939-1955*, Hodder & Stoughton, London.

W.K. Hancock, *Smuts 1 The Sanguine Years, 1870-1919*, Cambridge University Press, 1962.

W.K. Hancock, *Smuts 2 The Fields of Force 1919-1950*, Cambridge University Press, 1968.

K. Herd, *1922 The Revolt on the Rand*, Blue Crane Books, Johannesburg, 1966.

J.A. Hobson, *The War in South Africa, Its Causes and Effects*, James Nisbet and Co. Limited, 1900.

M. Hugo, *Die Kruger Ultimatum, Bienedell Uitgewers*, Pretoria sine dato.

J. Hunter, *Israeli Foreign Policy: South Africa and Central America*, South End Press, Boston, Massachusetts, 1987

D. Irving, *Churchill's War, The Struggle for Power*, Veritas Publishing Company Pty Ltd, Bullsbrook, Western Australia, 1987.

K. Ingham, *Jan Christian Smuts The Conscience of a South African*, Palgrave Macmillan, Johannesburg, 1986.

R.H. Kiernan, *General Smuts*, George G. Harrap & Company Ltd, London, 1944.

R. Kraus, *Old Master Thereof Jan Christian Smuts*, E.P. Dutton & Co. Inc., New York, 1944.

A.P. Laurie, *The Case for Germany. A Study of Modern Germany*, Internationaler Verlag, Berlin, 1939.

N. Levi, *Jan Smuts*, Longmans Green and Co., London, 1917.

J.A. Marais, *Die Era Verwoerd*, Aktuele Publikasies, Pretoria, 1992.

M.Mazower, *Jan Smuts misunderstood*, Princeton University Press, Princeton, New Jersey, 2009.

P. Meiring, *Smuts the Patriot*, Tafelberg Publishers Ltd, Cape Town, 1975.

S.G. Millin, *General Smuts*, Faber and Faber, Limited, London, 1938.

J.W. Muller, *Churchill as Peacemaker*, Woodrow Wilson Center Series and Cambridge University Press, 1997.

C. Mutwa, *My People: Writings of a Zulu Witchdoctor*, Penguin Books Ltd, Johannesburg, 1971.

C. Nordbruch, *The European Volunteers in the Anglo-Boer War 1899-1902*, Contact Publishers, Pretoria, 1999.

T. Pakenham, *The Boer War*, Jonathan Ball Publishers, London, 1979.

J.J. Peacock, *The Heel of the British Boot: The Deeper Meaning of the Second Anglo-Boer War*, Self-published, Cape Town, 2001.

P.J. Pretorius, *Volksverraad*, Libanon-Uitgewers, Mosselbaai, Western Cape, 1996.

C. Quigley, *Tragedy and Hope, A History of the World in Our Time*, The Macmillan Company, New York, 1966.

F.W. Reitz, *A Century of Wrong*, BiblioBazaar, Charleston, South Carolina, 2007.

F. Richter, *Vlug Vir Die Strafgerig*, Libanon- Uitgewers, Mosselbaai, Western Cape, 1995.

M.E. Rothman, *My Beskeie Deel – 'n Outobiografiese Vertelling*, Tafelberg, Kaapstad, 1972.

L. Scholtz, *Why the Boers Lost the War*, Palgrave Macmillan, London, 2005.

T.E.W. Schumann, *The Abdication of the White Man*, Tafelberg Uitgewers, 1963.

T. & D. Shearing, *General Smuts and his long ride*, Anglo-Boer War commemoration, 1999-2002, Self-published, Sedgefield, Western Cape, 2000.

J.C. Smuts (Jnr.), *Jan Christian Smuts*, Cassell & Company Ltd, Cape Town, 1952.

J.C. Smuts (Snr.), *Greater South Africa Plans For A Better World The Speeches of General The Right Honourable J.C. Smuts*, Truth Legion, Johannesburg, 1940.

J.C. Smuts (Snr.), *Holism and Evolution*, The Macmillan Company, New York, 1926.

O. Spengler, *The Decline of the West*, Alfred A. Knopf, Inc., Munich, 1926.

R.P. Stevens, *Weizmann and Smuts A Study in Zionist Co-operation*, Institute of Palestine Studies, Beirut, 1975.

R.Steyn, *Jan Smuts: Unafraid of Greatness*, Jonathan Ball Publishers, Cape Town, 2015.

P.C. Swanepoel, *General Jan Smuts: Was he on our Side in the Anglo-Boer War?* , Self-published, Pretoria, 2012.

A.F.B. Williams, *Botha Smuts and South Africa*, Hodder and Stoughton, London, 1946.

W.B. Worsfold, *Lord Milner's Work in South Africa From its Commencement in 1897 to the Peace of Vereeniging in 1902, Containing Hitherto Unpublished Information*, London, John Murray, 1906.

Index

A

H

I

J

K

L

Lansdowne, Lord Henry 17
Laurie, Dr. Arthur Pillans 55-56
League of Nations 3, 40
Leyds, Dr. Willem Johannes 23
Lloyd, Arthur Wynell 30
Locarno Treaty, 47
London Convention 15

M

MacDonald, Prime Minister Ramsay 64
Macrum, Charles E. 20
Majuba, battle of 15
Malan, Dr. Daniel Francois 33, 52, 61, 70
Malan, Hans 12
Malherbe, Prof. Mortie 57
Mandel, Georges 39
Mantoux, Etienne 39
Maritz, General Manie 33
Marks, Sammy 8
Millin, Sarah 13
Milner, Sir Alfred 9, 12-15, 54

N

National Convention 31
National Party 32, 49
Neser, Japie 28
Nettleton, Frank 44
Nooitgedacht, battle of 23

O

O'Connor, Captain Patrick 18
Oppenheimer, Sir Ernest 35, 44
Oppenheimer, Harry Frederick 61-62
Ossewa-Brandwag 56-57

P

Passfield, Lord Sidney 64
Peel Commission 64
SS Peru 30
Phillips, Sir Lionel 8-9
Pirow, Oswald 50, 53

Stoffberg, T.C. 4
Strakosch, Sir Henry 43-45
Styria 23
Swanepoel, Lieutenant General Piet 10, 15, 25, 27

T

Trotsky, Leon 33

U

Uitlanders 8, 10-11
SS Umgeni 33
Unionist Party 47
United Nations 3, 60-61
United Party 49, 62
US Federal Reserve Bank 42, 49, 58
USS Quincy 58

V

Van Rensburg, Dr. Johannes Frederik Janse 56
Vereeniging, Treaty of 28
Versailles, Treaty of 38-40, 54, 63
Verwoerd, Dr. H.F. 57, 61, 69-70
Victoria College 4
Von Czernin, Ottkar 38
Von Heydebreck, Colonel Joachim, 34
Von Lettow-Vorbeck, General Paul Emil 35-36
Von Mensdorff, Count Albert 38
Vorster, Balthazar Johannes 56-57

W

Weichardt, Louis 56
Weizmann, Dr. Chaim 63-65
Wessels, Commandant Piet 25
Whitman, Walt 5
Wilson, President Woodrow 38-40

Made in the USA
Middletown, DE
15 December 2019